Letters in a Bottle

A Legacy of Lockdown

Art Lester

Dim Lantern Press~LONDON

Copyright © 2020 by Art Lester

All rights reserved. No part of this publication may be reproduced, distributed or transmitted in any form or by any means, without prior written permission.

Letters in a Bottle/ Art Lester -- 1st ed.

ISBN 9798585660955

Cover design by Steven Appleby

For all the patient beachcombers
out looking for starfish

CONTENTS

Foreword
Sheltering on the Shore   1
The Covid Crucible   9
The Metaphorical Mask   15
Getting and Spending in the New Normal   20
Becoming Other-wise   26
Why Did the Chicken Cross the Road?   32
Working without a Net   38
Freedom is a Word I Rarely Use   45
What We do not Know   51
Breathe   57
Scaling the Wall   62
Coming Unstuck   68
Row, Row, Row Your Boat   74
Spiral of Violence   80
Starfish Fools   86
Finding Your Spring   93
Hunch Theology   99
Do the Right Thing   104
Paying Attention   110
Smile, Stupid   116
An Attitude of Gratitude   122
2020 Vision   128
We Have Lived So Long without the Holy   134
Frequently Asked Questions   140
Remembering the Future   146

FOREWORD

It was the Ides of March, 2020.

We had been hearing rumblings of an approaching pandemic for weeks. There was something about the atmosphere of the regular church service that hinted at strange times ahead. We didn't know then that we would be forced to suspend services for up to a year.

What followed was a general "shelter in place" order, which we have come to know as the First Lockdown. Regular attendees of the church were scattered like pigeons in the park. At first there was little or no communication between us, except for the occasional phone call.

The weather was stubbornly balmy. It didn't seem to fit the mood of foreboding that lay over us all. I heard that some churches were operating by way of Zoom services. We decided to follow suit, and in April, I recorded a sermon for the Paris Fellowship.

Sitting alone in a room, preaching to an iPhone, is not something I had training in all those years ago. Sermons are meant to be a kind of one-sided conversation with an audience. The preacher can read the faces of his or her victims, shortening, repeating, or just shutting up when the moment calls for it. But here we all were, marooned in our separate spaces, and even separate times. It reminded me of something, but I couldn't put my finger on it. Then it occurred to me.

Those sermons were like the messages shipwrecked sailors put into bottles. They are cast adrift, subject to tides and time, bobbing ceaselessly until the unlikely moment when someone picks them up on a beach.

With the help of some friends, we began preparing letters in bottles every Sunday. Though we were not allowed to open our doors to the public, we could legally gather a small crew of people to record a reasonable facsimile of a service. We began in May, as soon as lockdown restrictions were eased a bit, and kept it up for the next six months.

I'm grateful to the members of the crew: Steve, the director and cameraman, Lol, the singer and key grip, Gill and Will, whose wonderful piano music helped glue the services together, and Jim and Peter, newsletter editor and committee member, respectively, whose loyal presence gave me someone to look at while trying to preach.

And I'm grateful to you, for finding this bottle in the sand.

--Art Lester
November, 2020

WEEK ONE

Sheltering on the Shore

If I was where you are now, the first thing I'd do is look around at all your faces. Try to see everyone. Then I'd say what sounds like an ordinary greeting, but has now taken on a new depth and meaning: "How are you doing?"

Some of you might be brave and answer. But I'm guessing you wouldn't be saying, "Fine, thank you," the way we usually do. Because the things we usually do don't seem to apply at the moment. Something has shifted in our private and common life. Something has happened that it will take a long time to fully understand.

We have become vulnerable.

Do you remember the Road Runner cartoons? Wile E. Coyote spends his life chasing the mad bird, who constantly outwits him. Picture the scene where, just at the point of catching up with the Road Runner, Wile E misjudges a turn and winds up running off a cliff. But he is so fixated on his errand that he doesn't notice that he is running in thin air. It is only when he looks down that he sees reality, and it is only then that he falls.

Something like that is what has happened to us. It has happened to culture stars and prime ministers, tycoons and peasants. We thought our feet were on *terra firma*, but we've found that we were walking in air. The world we had constructed for ourselves—comfortable for some, less so for others—has changed beyond recognition.

We have become vulnerable.

As shocking as it all is, we should remember that we have always been vulnerable. Think about it: we are born helpless, without fins or scales or claws. We have the longest period of helplessness of any species. Without near total support, we die. And we sense that. When our nurturing parent leaves our side, even for a moment, we scream in what is nothing less than existential terror.

Then, throughout the longest spell of maturing of any species, we gradually evolve coping mechanisms. We build little nests of relationships and create stories that give us comfort and security. We buy insurance policies, invent antibiotics, store up mementoes and trophies on the mantelpiece, and seal ourselves into a coherent world view, reinforced by religion. If we are lucky, we may traverse an entire lifetime without having to see that we are walking in air. Or, perhaps if we are even luckier, we might have the opportunity to see clearly what this pandemic is urging us to see.

We have become vulnerable. We ARE vulnerable.

Not so long ago, when such things were still possible, I conducted a funeral for someone I didn't know. It was an elderly woman, a friend of a friend of a friend. As always, I had someone write a short bio so that I could make the occasion less abstract. As I read the words, I

LESTER

felt that I was learning about an "ordinary" life, and yet finding it much more than ordinary. The piece was warm in my hands. It was shot through with love.

It rained buckets outside. The family wept. My own voice broke as I pressed the button for the final curtain, something I have done many, many times before. And, as always, I wished I could find the words, some magic charm that would clear the air of the grief, anger and guilt that so often hangs around funeral services.

After the service, the daughter of the dead woman grabbed my sleeve and said, "You make me feel so much better about all this." And, as always, I knew that there was really nothing you could say that would change things profoundly. But that—maybe—standing next to people in extreme circumstances was better than any great words you might utter.

Recently, I remembered a story from the Sufi tradition. A little wave is rolling across the sea when a scary thought occurs to him. He turns and says to a big wave, "I think I see a beach ahead. I'm scared. What will happen to me?" The big wave answers, "That will always be how you feel until you remember that you are really the ocean."

It made me think of a statement by Friedrich Nietzsche. He said that the world contained just three kinds of people. There are those who build sandcastles on the beach, unaware that the sea will dissolve and reclaim them. There are those who, knowing that the life of a sandcastle is fleeting and insecure, decide not to even

3

try. And there is a third type: those who, knowing that the sandcastle cannot possibly survive the tide, do it anyway.

We all know people of each type. In fact, we might say we have been all three kinds of people at various times in our lives. As a young person, when the world seems easy and fun, and time is not an issue, we hatch great plans and attack the world with enthusiasm. We know intellectually that nothing is forever, but we can brandish the words like a magic charm: "Not yet."

But sometimes life affronts us. A pandemic ceases to be a sci-fi concept and becomes a hard reality. People who are just like us die. Our cherished hopes seem to ebb away in the slow drip of days, and the comforting spell of the ordinary—the world of mortgages, vacations and pension funds—are chipped away. Then it may seem that the best thing to do is say, "What's the use, anyway?" So, we turn away from our sandcastle projects and march to the droning beat of the necessary and the next.

But if we are lucky, and blessed with the right kind of temperament, we can shrug off the dread of the inevitable and get stuck in again. Get out the pail and shovel, squat in the sand and begin to build again. Turrets and moats and a flag on top, fashioned from an ice cream wrapper. The best and bravest among us may even stay till sundown, and watch as the waves reclaim the sand and the project is dissolved. That's when we have the opportunity to see that nothing is destroyed except an idea, a small mirage that comes and goes. The sand remains, each grain rearranged in accordance with another, grander plan.

The whole of the mystical literature of virtually all religious traditions has the same simple truths to offer. Put in easy language, it goes like this: we are not who we think we are. The reality we have forged for ourselves is a kind of temporary nest, like those made by migratory birds. Because we have forgotten our true selves, we cling to the straws and sticks we forage from the landscape around us. We strive to make the nest as strong and solid as possible. We reinforce it with things that seem to be permanent, shore up our positions with institutions and relationships, and set about weathering the storms of confusion.

The teacher Meher Baba put it this way (and I have to paraphrase): "Humanity will forever build illusory shelters on the shore of truth, until wave after wave of life drives their occupants onward."

Does that mean that even a thing as shocking as a pandemic might harbour benefits that we don't see—cannot see—when our shoreline shelters are intact? Is there some gift in the knowledge that we are vulnerable?

What is the dominant emotion shared by nearly everyone now? What motivates the bankers to leave New York City for the Hamptons in their droves? What turns the blessings of one's "golden years" into a blueprint of risk and withdrawal? What makes the heroic workers in ICU wards present grim faces to the TV cameras every night?

LETTERS IN A BOTTLE

The answer can be expressed in one word: *fear*. That fear that makes the infant scream when its mother leaves the room. The fear that drives us to build sandcastles of security, ringed in by relationships and guarded by opinions. Put baldly, the fear of non-existence, the fear of death.

Along with our clinging to worldly things, we have evolved other ruses to prevent the worst. We create religions in which we can accumulate merit like vouchers we can redeem for an unlikely extension of our earthly lives after death. We imagine that we can stay the same forever, as if we could pick up the sandcastle and move it to a place where there is no tide.

But even in these poor places of dogma, voices have often emerged that sing us a different sort of song. They say that before we took birth and after we have gone, we have always been. That while we live, our true existence is not arrested, only hidden. And that the way back is through the only force that can overcome fear: love.

It is love that appears when the misty mountain sunrise or the transporting strain of music breaks through the walls of the ordinary. It is love that is both joy and longing, mixed. And finally, it is love that makes you remember who you are.

We are never so vulnerable as when we love. When we dare to risk rejection, and ignore the ultimate inevitability of bereavement and loss. And it may be that the obverse is true: that when we are aware of our vulnerability, our capacity to love is enhanced. That may be why we have seen so many touching examples of generosity of spirit during this time of trouble. Why the health workers are able to go to work in overburdened wards, and the neighbours queue up to bring supplies to the elderly. It may just be that knowing directly how fleeting life can be energises our capacity to care.

I'll let you in on a secret. When people like me write sermons, what they say is meant not just for the listener, but for themselves. So, do I wake up at 5 a.m. and let the monsters of doubt and confusion, the ogres of small terrors, overtake me? You bet I do. But as I get older, the demons seem to get a bit weaker. Do I fear death? Of course I do, but, then I fear leaping into cold water, too.

What heartens and sustains me is that I have no deadline. Something has spoken to *me* in the night, saying that whether or not I see through the curtain before my little wave hits the beach, it really doesn't matter. If I am able to see through the sham reality I have so carefully constructed, fine. But if not, in time all that will be clear to me. Like the words of 1 Corinthians say, now I see through a glass darkly, but then face to face.

Because there is something else that the mystics say, something that never fails to bring me peace. Best expressed by Mother Julian of Norwich in these lines: "All is well, all shall be well, all manner of things shall be well."

So, I guess that means that whether we grasp the truth or not, everything is all right. Yes, really: nothing is

LETTERS IN A BOTTLE

broken; everything is accounted for. So lighten up, little wave: everything IS all right.

WEEK TWO

The Covid Crucible

I've been out a bit lately. For the first three months of lockdown, I did little more than walk my daily two miles around the neighbourhood, but since then I've been a few times to the little writing room I rent in Crystal Palace. I wear a mask, even when I don't get near anyone, and gloves for things like doorknobs.

There are some people on the street. A big queue at Sainsbury's. A coffee shop selling hot drinks to people on the kerb. The window cleaner, who is as much a fixture of the place as the twin radio towers, looking wistfully at the closed shop fronts. It all feels eerie, like a scene from a zombie movie. Other shops are opening now, so maybe that will pass. But I don't think I will ever feel that I'm completely back. Things have changed, and everything seems different. Different, but nearly the same, like in a dream.

Our last full service here in the church was on March 15th. I can recall joking that we should "beware the Ides of March." I felt then that something was about to change. It was like the moments before a storm, when the pressure of the air drops, and a kind of ominous silence occurs. We knew about the virus, and playfully used elbow bumps instead of handshakes, but we couldn't have known what lay ahead. Since then, we have been moved by unpredictable forces, like leaves swept downstream in a flood.

We may have thought that what we were facing was a short-term medical emergency, nothing as serious as earlier generations have faced with wars and depressions. At first, the isolation wasn't too bad, because we thought things would get back to normal soon. It has taken us a while to begin to understand that something much more profound is happening. That things might never be the same again.

Unemployment has reared its unfamiliar head. Endemic racial injustice we have left unaddressed for centuries has popped up. Things we thought were disasters, like Brexit, hardly get a mention in the press. The faces of politicians who have bored us for years have taken over the airways, doling out unlikely prescriptions from temporary lecterns. Some people set fire to things. Others topple statues of yesterday's heroes, today's villains. If you see your friends at all, they are framed in little squares on Zoom. Everything, everywhere, is telling us the same thing: something big is happening.

But why is all this stuff happening at once? Unattended issues of familial abuse, the newly exposed plight of single mothers, people without gardens or even balconies on which to catch a few sun rays, food banks running out of stock, cancer treatment suspended. All this, and everyone having a bad hair day that lasts for months. It is as if something very basic, something fundamental, has changed. Something underneath everything is being altered.

I look about for metaphors to address issues I can't grasp in detail. It is as if our lives were in a big container. And then something set a fire under it, and life began to boil. That led me to the idea that we're all stuck in a giant pot, and something has turned up the heat.

A crucible is a pot in which you boil things in order to change them. It is a way to refine metal. You get the ore very hot, to melting point. The impurities are separated out, while the valuable stuff remains. It can be poured into moulds, cooled, and made into ingots. The impurities are thrown away, onto slag heaps.

As you can see, I'm letting my taste for metaphors run a bit wild here. You can see that I'm saying that the long, insistent flame of the pandemic is beginning to separate what is important from what is not. In isolation, we have had time to see what is really valuable. We have watched as forces beyond our control have taken from us things we thought we needed. People have lost jobs, homes and relationships. There has been real suffering and death. But there has also been the loss of unimportant things, things that do belong on the slag heap. Things that we may not have noticed, have got used to. But also things that we simply have to discard if we are to have a future at all.

The crucible is ruthless. It heats up the true along with the false, the selfish along with the fair. Those who have been winners in the past have tasted failure. Those who have long brought up the rear in our competitive life game have suddenly got company. This levelling empowers the powerless even as it strips the powerful of their advantage. Just look in the streets of our cities. The phrase "We are all in this together" takes on a different tone. It is beginning to mean that the old systems of control and privilege are fading. That's the reason why the statue of the slaveowner Edward Colston ended up in Bristol Harbour.

The crucible has this function of purification. That's how gold was originally made pure enough to place value on its content. But there is a second function of the crucible, one used by alchemists in centuries past. A crucible is where you form an alloy; where you take things that are different, put them into a state at which both are equal, and let them combine. Copper and tin make bronze, nickel marries with silver. You can rub these discrete elements together all you like and not join them into something new. That takes the fiery element of the crucible.

The Sufi poet Rumi refers to this process in his metaphor about cooking chickpeas. When the chickpeas protest, Rumi tells them: "You think I'm torturing you. I'm giving you flavour, so that you can mix with spices and rice and become the lovely vitality of a human being. Remember when you drank rain in the garden? That was for this."

People used to joke that the only thing that would bring together all the nations of the world was a common enemy—meaning something like a Martian invasion. Astronomers have robbed us of this little fantasy. It now exists only in computer-generated films. Meanwhile, just such a common threat has sneaked up on us from behind. The links between environmental destruction and the emergence of new diseases have been made startlingly clear. If we needed a common threat, we've got it.

As the crucible cooks our familiar world, we may be able to look forward to a leaner, more stripped-down and—hopefully—a more equitable outcome. That metal which is pure in us is being refined, and the slag discarded. But an even more hopeful result is possible. We may just be able to join the disparate elements of tribe, nation and race into a more cohesive whole. This isn't discredited alchemical foolishness, but something more closely akin to scientific reality.

Did you know that the United States has a motto? Or it did have until 1956, when "In God We Trust" started appearing on paper money. The old one comes from the ancient Greek philosopher, Heraclitus. Translated into Latin, it's *e pluribus unum*. Out of many, one. The much-vaunted melting pot that Americans have laid claim to for so long now has a chance of becoming real.

We won't have a chance of returning to normal life—or perhaps any chance of life at all—until the vision of becoming one is at least partially realised. The "new

LETTERS IN A BOTTLE

normal" we keep hearing about may have emphasis on the first word, instead of the second. What was "normal" is now winding up on the slag heap. What is "new" may be just beginning to show.

Keep your eyes on the cooking pot.

WEEK THREE

The Metaphorical Mask

Jean-Paul Sartre, the wall-eyed existentialist philosopher, once told a story about a university professor, a mild-mannered man in his fifties, who stepped off a kerb one day in Paris and got hit by a bus. Passers-by rushed to his aid, to find that he was laughing. When asked why, with a badly broken leg, he found something so amusing, he replied: "At last—something has happened to *me*!"

Some of us may be able to identify with the professor. Middle-class white people of my generation—with a few exceptions—have sailed through life. We have had an unrivalled era of peace between the large nations. We have had a constantly growing economy with plenty of opportunity for education and career. We have immersed ourselves in self-cultivation and pleasure. We thought wars, economic collapses and deadly pandemics were just good movie themes, best enjoyed with popcorn. We thought that things were meant to be that way. Of course, there have been private tragedies, but the world we thought we inhabited was always tending toward enhanced freedom, wealth and happiness.

Then, one day in March 2020, we stepped off the kerb. Without warning, we had bumped straight into a crisis.

Until recently, it was fashionable among preachers and motivational speakers to point to the Chinese character for the word *crisis*, and to claim that it was formed of the separate words for "danger" and "opportunity". Further study has revealed that to be wide of the mark. The first part, it is true, reflects danger. But the second part isn't about opportunity. It simply means what everyone who has ever been in a crisis already knows: things are going to change.

Sometimes a crisis is imagined as a crossroads or a forking path. But if you stay closer to the real meaning of the word, what you get is more like a T-junction. The road you have been travelling runs out. You have a choice between turning left or right. But there is no chance of continuing in the direction you were heading in before.

The more I hear about something called the "new normal", the way things will be after this pandemic finally ends, the clearer it is to me that much of what we have come to rely upon as permanent elements of life is destined for change. I'm not thinking of the death of the handshake or even the stockpiling of ventilators for the future. I'm speaking from an intuition—not unique to me—that things we have not yet considered are on their way in or on their way out. I'm not a prophet, but this is becoming more and more obvious all the time. All around us, voices are saying that there are now two directions left to us. One way leads to a dialled-back, gentler, greener society. The other to nationalism and surveillance.

We have been landed with a bump right square in the middle of history. This event is enormous. In the narrative of our lives, this is not just a comma. 9/11 was a comma. The so-called Great Recession was a comma. This is a semicolon, if not a full stop. And the sooner we take this on board, the better off we'll be.

If that sounds dire, I apologise. Nobody really likes change. You can make children cry by altering things. Ditto old people. A kid likes to hear the same bedtime story over and over again, and so do people like me. But what we may forget is that the entirety of our lives has been about change and adaptation. Every spurt of growth has demanded change: change of home, change of employment, change of partner, change in physical ability.

Now the changes carried on the ill wind of Covid-19 have begun to make themselves evident. We will experience big changes in travel. Cinemas and high street shops will close, altering our familiar neighbourhoods. You may meet the love of your life as a two-dimensional image onscreen. But what will change the most—what must change the most—is a mindset we have lived with for all our lives.

Ironically, a big change in our future attitudes may be reflected in what you might consider its least likely form—the mask. Now, I don't know how many of you have started wearing face coverings. After all, they're not required in the UK, based on some curious logic of our leaders. But after months of theorising on both sides of the issue, it has emerged that masks do help prevent the spread of Covid-19. And I have come to believe that mask-wearing is the perfect metaphor for how we must change.

It may be true that the mask offers little protection for the wearer. But it's also true that by blocking respiratory droplets from infecting people around you, you are helping to stop the spread of the disease. Helping others, in other words. Sadly, the issue of mask wearing has become a divisive political one, even leading to occasional violence in America. Non-wearers, like the American president, might ask, "Why should I? What's in it for me?", thereby illustrating what needs changing.

Our economy, and to a great extent our culture, are based on the significance of this question. Since the days of Adam Smith we have accepted that individual (let's just say "selfish") desires, magnified by competition, would ultimately enrich everyone. Kind of an automatic function, perhaps ordained by God's "unseen hand", as Smith wrote.

If there was not already a plethora of evidence to debunk this point of view, the pandemic has made it all too clear. Who, besides the elderly, trapped in nursing homes, is dying? The answer is edifying. It is the poorest, the least paid, the workers in the dirtiest jobs, and—

outrageously—the darkest skinned. In an "I'm all right, Jack" society, you can fly away to your private island, isolate yourself behind high walls and pay the workers peanuts to do the dirty work.

None of this is really new. Voices since Old Testament prophets like Amos have told us that our fate depends upon how we treat each other: the stranger, the homeless and the weak. What the pandemic has done is underscore the depth of our miscalculation, our self-centredness. The phrase "we are all in this together" has been hollow as long as misfortune was individual; now that we are all vulnerable, it takes on new meaning. It derives straight from the first big question in the Bible: "Am I my brother's keeper?"

Just as in so many large issues of our time, we might feel too helpless to do anything meaningful. So here's my suggestion: put your mask on. If you have one handy, wherever you are, go ahead and put it on now. This is a mask that is not a means of self-concealment, but a measure of self-revelation. Put it on, even if you're not going anywhere or seeing anybody. Don't do it defiantly, or politically. Let its scratchiness and stuffiness affect you. Do it with love. Let it tell you something you may have been able to ignore before now: we really are all in it together. Your fate and mine are so closely interlinked as to be indistinguishable. Because it's true, you know: You and I are not "we" at all; we are one.

To which I say, AMEN.

WEEK FOUR

Getting and Spending in the New Normal

What's the first thing you learn to say in a foreign language on holiday? Yes, "Hello" and "Thank you", with "Where is the toilet?" pretty close behind. Then it's that indispensable phrase: "How much is it?"

Maybe you're like me. You don't like to talk much about money. It seems sort of, ... well, vulgar. Maybe that's spiritual, or maybe it's just being prissy. A famous minister once said that if you forced everybody in a church service to choose between revealing how much money they make and taking off their clothes, the whole congregation would look like a nudist colony.

Lots of us believe that spirituality has nothing much to do with money. There's that old divide: God and something called "mammon". I always wondered what mammon might be; it sounded like a cut of ham to me. It turns out that it comes to us from the Aramaic—the language Jesus used. The word was *mamona*, meaning "riches", especially in a negative sense, as in "You cannot serve God and Mammon."

That is probably why certain religious vows involve poverty, as well as chastity and obedience. None of those things sound very palatable or rewarding. Poverty especially. Having seen a bit of it in the so-called Third World, it's hard for me to think of it as anything other than the cruel and demeaning thing it is.

When I worked at village level in some poor countries, I saw up close how lack of money influences every aspect of life. Yes, children can survive a few missing meals. Papa can walk six miles to work in a sugar cane mill because he hasn't got 20 cents for a bus. A mother with a headache can do without aspirin. But a hungry child can't learn. A father can bring about disaster by suffering something as simple as a sprained ankle. And Mum can't heal her brain tumour with the incantations of a local healer. Those actual examples caused me to realise that people like us can only ever be *broke*; poverty is something entirely different.

Money appears all the time in the Good Book; you might even say it is a preoccupation. For all that this is true, we seem to have neglected it in many of our inherited moral structures. There is plenty about sex, but not a lot about money. Not that it's not on all our minds. Why else would we have so many names for it: moolah, lolly, dough, bread, wedge, bucks and quid, brass, cash, fold, "the readies", loot, spondoolies, splash, shekels, and so on and on?

The old fairy tale says that money is stored energy. You put in a certain amount of work, say growing pumpkins. You can't eat them all at harvest, and anyway you'd get sick of yellow soup and pies pretty soon. So, you trade them for some coins that are easier to carry around, and you can exchange them for somebody else's turnips or eggs. If you don't have any place to grow pumpkins, then you work. If you're lucky enough to have a lot of coins, you can have others do the work for you, multiplying wealth quietly in the marketplace, while you sleep late or cultivate your appetites. That little round thing in your pocket is like a small battery, ready to discharge its energy when you want it. Simple, right?

Nope. That reductionistic little sketch of a complex process is one that might be told by a jolly billionaire to his grandchildren. It's the kind of story loved by people with a lot of money, and not so admired by those without any. It represents money as a neutral phenomenon, working as automatically as, say, photosynthesis in a plant. What it leaves out is all the sweat, toil and blood of history—the point where money touches human life.

One of my all-time heroes was E. F. Schumacher, who wrote the little book "Small is Beautiful". It inspired me to leave the US and study at a college in Sussex. What moved me particularly was the subtitle: "Economics as if People Mattered". The ideas expressed in the book were radical back in the 1970s, when he wrote it, but it seems to me that we may have begun to grow into understanding it and taking it on.

The Rabbi Jesus had a lot to say about money, too. On one of his turns around the temple he saw a widow paying two annas for a pigeon—the smallest acceptable sacrifice in the gigantic charnel house that was the centre of Hebrew worship. He made the point that her sacrifice was greater than its cash value because it represented all she had.

The fact that this was news to his disciples—enough so as to record the event—illustrates the fact that God was being seen at that time as a kind of cosmic pawnbroker; what pleased Him was pounds, shillings and pence. Jesus was painting a different picture of worship, God, and of money itself. He was relating it not to the marketplace, but to the subjective condition of human beings.

If money isn't that simple, neutral thing we thought it was, then what is it? A Spanish finance minister, resigning from his post during the 1980s, said this: "Spain isn't a country anymore; it's a casino." Meaning that his old socialist attitudes had been outraged to find that investment is just another name for gambling. Money had become something that wasn't like stored energy anymore, but chips in a vast crap game, making winners out of some and losers out of everyone else.

Nobody much is listening to Jesus or any of the world's wise people these days. It's easy to shut out all those prophetic noises he was making about money and the poor because it was long ago and oh so far away.

Or maybe I should say that no one was listening before the present economic crisis engulfed us. Things are more complicated now; we don't know yet how things are going to turn out. And it's not just poor old Jesus: there's not so much interest in the words of the Buddha, either, with his call for "right livelihood". As for the Islamic world, they have found any number of ingenious devices to get around Mohammed's ban on usury—the collection of interest. But it's still possible to claim that the stock market will recover, and that we will once again believe those fairy tales about stored energy and gambling tokens.

I think we are faced here with a tantalising idea. Millions of formerly coping people are now flat broke. It must be the case that we will now have to think again, in our "new normal", about how we get and spend money. We must earn it, save it, make it work. We must also try to understand where it comes from, what it costs ourselves or someone else, and make informed decisions. And maybe reach beyond even this, to a spiritual dimension, overcoming the old God and Mammon paradox at last, to ask "Why?" about the process and to make it register with a growing awareness of the earth and our place within it. To move beyond the short term, or the medium term, to the real term profit of life on Planet Earth.

I think the new normal language will change, too. Instead of the question, "How much do you *make*?", we might be asking, "How much do you *earn*?" The difference seems paltry, but it is not. It speaks to the reassignment of morality to money. *How* we come by our daily crust will be important in a new economic reality. If we are blessed, making the easy buck will become a sign of shame. When we grow up, we will understand that commerce is not a private game, but an act of morality, counted in pumpkins.

This storm, someday, will have passed. We will find ourselves, like Robinson Crusoe, on the beach with the scraps of the ship we have lost. It will be up to us to put them back together, to make something new from the wreckage of the old. It is then that we can decide what wealth will do to us, what it can do for us.

It will be exciting. Will we start again enslaving ourselves and others with the bunkum of a constantly growing economy, seeking to squeeze more comfort and pleasure from a finite world than it can easily give? Or can this uninvited break from the mad tune of the fiddler let us think again, plan again, care again?

Watch this space.

WEEK FIVE

Becoming Other-wise

When I worked in Botswana in the 1980s, I lived in a centre for refugees of the scourge called *apartheid*. My friends were all black South Africans whose lives had been ruined by racism and oppression. Some of them had been tortured. One had come through a hole in the fence with three bullets in his body. I read Nelson Mandela and Steve Biko and talked freedom. I got mad at my employers, the Quakers, because they wouldn't let ANC members stay at the centre. The movement believed in violence, said the local members of the meeting.

Having made my bones as a civil rights protestor during the sixties, I had a very low opinion of white South Africans. I thought I knew all about their racist world view because of my upbringing in the American South. I say that in sorrow because I was wrong. I found out just how wrong when I got back to the UK. There, I met a young minister of the Dutch Reformed Church, Patrick, a man who, until three years previously, had preached the gospel of apartheid. Literally finding in Bible passages how God intended black people to be the servants of the white, superior race. He had been passionate about this, and—as he explained—he was able to hold this view because he saw blacks as objects, not people. Objects could be loaded onto trucks and sent into the barren mountains. They could be forced to carry passports in their own country; even—if they got frisky—be shot in the street. And all of this could be justified by the Bible.

One day, back in South Africa, Patrick confiscated a banned copy of "My Life with Martin Luther King", by Coretta Scott King, from a student. Amused, he began to read. Here's what he told me of that moment: "Art, the government were so right to ban that book. By the end of the first chapter my life was beginning to change. Not because of any greatness on the part of Martin Luther King—I couldn't see that yet. But because it suddenly occurred to me that King was actually a *person*—just like me." He spent days praying and thinking, and when he was done, preached an anti-apartheid sermon from his own pulpit. He was sacked, virtually defrocked, and evicted from the parsonage. His family reviled him. He joined the fledgling UDF (United Democratic Front) and became a non-violent activist. Finally, he went into exile. He was one of the most remarkable people I've ever met.

His appearance in my life did the same thing for me as the book had for him. I saw him not as a Boer fascist, but as a person, just like me. He helped me realise that when you hate people, you don't really see them; they're just objects to be manipulated or ignored. They have no independent existence; they are simply *others*.

This process of "othering" happens when we allow ourselves the dirty little secret pleasure of a racial epithet. It happens when the behaviour of someone "foreign" to us is used as an example of their inferiority, as when an Asian jumps a queue. It happens when we interpret body language and dress style as defiance of "decent" behaviour. It happens when we count the towels on the beach chairs that some Germans have left or avoid three young black men on a street corner. Every time it happens, a tiny seed of hate is sown. Not by the Trump administration or the president of Russia; by us.

I'm going to confess something to you. I do it in the hope that it will help empower you. I've been an opponent of racism all my adult life, after starting out in a "genteel" racist background in the Deep South. My father's granddad was the owner of a turpentine plantation with 66 enslaved people. As I grew up, I rejected all that. I became a marcher in the civil rights demos of the 1960s, and have spent years in Africa, where all my friends were dark-skinned. And yet, sometimes, my moral fatigue overcomes me, on a crowded bus, say, and an ugly thought, together with what I really know is an unfair generalisation, begins to struggle for domination in my head. I might mutter, "Typical". I can suppress it, overrule it, beat myself up for having it. But, God help me, I can't deny that it is lying doggo in my subconscious, like a snake beside the path.

I said I hope what I confessed might empower you. Here's what I mean: since the killing of George Floyd, people have been more than ever exercised by the issue of racism. Demonstrations and counter-demonstrations have stolen the thunder even from the terrible progress of the pandemic through our populations. There has been a tendency amongst liberals like us to express what has been called "virtue signalling". Saying things like, "Not me— I haven't got a racist bone in my body. Some of my best friends are black." Someone who is virtue signalling is distancing himself or herself from the evil seen in others, as well as from the awareness of the unfairly stacked equation of white privilege. Targets of this are fascist cops and right-wing politicians, mainly. But also people who haven't become as "woke" as the signaller. It is a form of self-reassurance that, ironically, helps promote the process of "othering", which is at the root of what we call racism in the first place.

Some thinkers have correctly identified racism as an extreme form of "othering", something most humans do: identifying allies and enemies. "Othering" would have been a survival characteristic in a tribal world. At its root is the competition for resources, leading on to the exploitation of others for wealth. Slavery was its finest flower. Discrimination in social and economic affairs is its favoured descendant.

Scientists now tell us that there is really no such thing as race. All members of the species *Homo sapiens* are essentially the same. To take a lesson from our best friend, the dog, we can see that it doesn't matter to a Great Dane if a playmate is a Chihuahua. A dog is a dog. But it is handy for "othering" humans to use skin colour, especially, but also language as a marker. It is easy to identify as "other" someone with a different colour skin.

But if all those years of trying haven't taken that ugly tendency from me, educated, enlightened me, what is there to be done?

This time of crisis has given us what seems to be a new opportunity to chuck some of the sins of the past overboard. The possibility of new laws, new spending priorities, and new treatment of minorities in film and other high-profile fields. That is indeed necessary, and we can all agree that it is right. But—is it enough?

I often wonder if you can make yourself love your enemy, as some half-forgotten great soul once suggested. So now I think that maybe the answer is more about being willing to explore the position of the other, rather than waiting for floods of sympathetic tears and feeling your heart go all pitty-pat. Maybe we can't feel emotion that swells in our breasts when an unlucky foreigner or underprivileged slum-dweller winds up afoul of our laws. But maybe we can understand it a bit and make judgements about it based on what is ultimately helpful instead of wallowing in self-justified anger.

The trick is to learn how to make eye contact with him, rather than kiss him or slap him. You might say, to become other-wise. Not easy—not easy at all—but I believe it is the only way through this seemingly never-ending round of slaps and kisses. When we expunge the poison of "othering", we make the future possible. Make it possible in ways that until now have seemed increasingly unlikely.

And maybe, if we intend it hard enough, that snake in the grass might just curl up and die, or at least shrink a bit. The only war that we should be waging, as the spiritual master, Meher Baba, said, is the one between our best and worst selves. That takes effort, and will, and—yes—the rudiments of love.

So what do you say? Shall we start here? Shall we do what we know we must? Go out of here with the intention of loving someone that we cannot love? Maybe it will be a foreigner; maybe a violent kid driven mad by bad treatment; maybe even someone who has hurt us. Certainly an *other*. Not loving in any phoney or hypocritical way. Just trying to put a thumb on the scales in the direction of a better world. We're the only ones who can do it, you know.

Yes, that's what I said: we're the *only* ones.

WEEK SIX

Why Did the Chicken Cross the Road?

Early in the Lockdown, back in March, I got a call from someone I didn't know. She identified herself as Linda, and it took me a moment to realise that she was the wife of my friend and loyal cab driver, Len.

She was crying. Through the sobs, I got her message. Len had become ill a couple of weeks after they returned from a Spanish holiday. He went into hospital, then intensive care. They phoned Linda to say that he was dying, but that she couldn't visit him because of the risk of infection. Three hours later, he was dead.

I've had a number of such calls over the years. I think they call me because they are hoping for an explanation, as well as comfort. One thing they have in common, whatever the circumstances, is what I think of as a prayer; they want to know *why*.

They don't mean the name of the disease, or the number plate of the other driver in the accident. They have no particular interest in "underlying conditions", or the blood alcohol level of the second driver. They want to know *why* this has happened. Something that has eluded the calm narrative of their lives, something unexpected, something inexplicable. I believe they know

I can't give them an answer, but the question has too much mass to ignore. They are like people standing on a cliff's edge screaming into the night, toward an unknown God.

In the last few years, we have been treated to a welter of popular theories from physicists, mathematicians, even biologists, like Richard Dawkins for example. In their furious need to explain everything—or, perhaps to explain it *away*—they have done what can only be seen as metaphysical claim-jumping. Hence, we have autopsies and electrode experiments looking for what has been called the "God gland" in the human brain— the reason *why* the concept of God uniquely occurs to human beings.

I'm not anti-scientific. How could I be, in these grim days when we hang on every word the scientists utter? I'm certainly not opposed to the technology that—for example—saved the sight of my right eye a few years ago and has made marvellous new hip joints for a lot of my friends. What wearies me is the misuse of that three-letter word that science enthusiasts employ so readily when they say, "This is *why* such and such a phenomenon takes place." I feel that they don't mean "why" at all, but a complicated version of "how".

The ancient Greek philosopher Aristotle described four kinds of causality. I forget the first ones, but the last two are very interesting, and should perhaps be integrated into the curriculum of any budding scientist. They are "efficient cause" and "final cause". Efficient cause is linked to the idea of agency: what it is that happens to make something else happen. The old joke expresses this perfectly: "Why did the chicken cross the road?" The reply, "To get to the other side" is both funny and unsatisfying, but it's as far as efficient cause can take you.

What Aristotle called "final cause" is a bit more complex. We may try the scientific route, describing and circumscribing the stages of an event. But what we want to know is way outside the scope of scientific speculation—at least as we know it so far. Final cause would answer the question "Why was it necessary for the car to crash?" In other words, the meaning and significance of the event, not just a description of it.

When the scientific method becomes the single lodestone of human knowledge, as it seems to have done lately, we are stuck one level too far back. We get caught up in an endless loop of "how?", when what our hearts long for is an answer to the bigger question: "why?" I remember one Christmas Eve of my childhood asking my father why a furniture truck had just struck and killed my dog. He began to answer by saying that maybe old Tim had grown too deaf to hear the truck as it approached. But I wanted more, and asked him again, "But why?" Catching my meaning, that most plaintive human query of all, he said, "Son, I don't know."

When I have been called upon to deal with people who have suddenly become bereaved, I go through all the things I was taught in counselling and ministry training. I sit with them in their grief as much as I am able, and try to offer the pale comfort of another person's presence. It does help, for sure, when the grief and shock are raw. But it's never very long until that same question emerges, either spoken or implied; the one question that lies at the very heart of the human condition: *Why?*

There are many quick remedies for this universal problem, ways of distracting oneself with hobbies, love affairs, patriotism, new cars. We are familiar with all this—we all do it. It may work for a while, may offer some soothing music to drown out the drone of the constant questions we might hear if we listened: *Why? What does it all mean? What's the point?*

How hard we work to avoid hearing this question! How much we fear its being asked, and how we resist when it snatches us out of bed or descends upon us in a doctor's surgery, or seems to float in the air of autumn like the leaves from the un-protesting trees. But sometimes, when we simply cannot avoid it, the question grips us. This moment is not just an affliction but a gift. Just as crises may bear a secret benefit of opportunity, I think that the question of meaning, or the dread of its absence, carries with it something of our birth right, a treasure waiting to be discovered.

I said earlier that I considered the question "why?" to be a kind of prayer. I think it may in fact turn out to be the root of all prayer, in that it is a plea for meaning. When you turn toward something you cannot see, and whimper or shout out "Why?", you are acting as if there were someone to hear, and perhaps to answer. It's as if something basic in you understands that, beneath the raw confusion of life, a floor of meaning exists.

Seen in this way, the prayer "Why?" is not just a cry for help. It is an authentication of meaning in the universe, an unintended statement of praise. The question not only implies that meaning must somehow exist; it is itself an expression of that meaningfulness.

Sceptics might argue that we humans are projecting onto an empty universe our own needs for reason and order. Seen like that, it is no different from the other human attributes we insist upon as traits of a non-existent, fairy-tale God. If human life is ordered and reasonable, then God must be also. But I would say that the human experience is anything but ordered and reasonable. The plain fact that such qualities are imputed to God speak of the shape of that archetype of reason and order that lies submerged within each of us, as a birth-right.

Put simply, I believe that there is an irreducible understanding within each of us that life is not random, that we are more than pinballs colliding in an alien cosmic game. Crises evoke this in us. They make us turn our faces to the unknown and demand an explanation. They make us pray.

The answer to that kind of prayer comes in an unexpected way. Instead of receiving a chapter and verse response to the question, we may learn to be calm in the mystery. If we are not so easily mollified, we may remain angry. But this again implies that something, somewhere, holds an answer—because, otherwise, who exactly would we be mad at?

That old joke may turn out to be as subtle as a Zen riddle, a *ko-an*. Not satisfied with the answer given, we are required to dig down a bit. Why DID the chicken cross the road?

There must have been something on the other side. There must be something on the other side.

WEEK SEVEN

Working without a Net

Do you ever hear songs or phrases that seem to stick with you without any apparent reason? Something you may not quite understand but which somehow lodges in your head? One such for me was a song by Waylon Jennings, a country and western singer. To be honest, I'm not even a fan.

"We don't even know where we are.
They say that we're circling a star.
Well, I'll take their word—I don't know.
I'm dizzy, so maybe it's so."

In those simple lines, our biggest human mystery stands revealed. As a child, I used to love looking up into the stars and getting a sense of the immensity of the universe. But sometime along the way—I'm not sure exactly when—that very immensity began to seem oppressive. And as I learned more of what the super scientists like Brian Cox have to say, that big, interesting universe out there started to seem alien and threatening. It's one thing to sit securely on a fixed bit of immovable earth and wonder about the stars, as the ancients must have done. But it's another thing altogether when you become aware that we too are swirling in vast, empty space, with no up and no down.

In the village in southern Spain where I have a little cottage, the cemetery sits on top of the highest hill. And next to it is a gigantic rock, the size of a freight car, which is entirely painted white, as it has been for centuries. This is to serve as a marker for Jesus, when he flies over to raise the dead from their graves. They are taking no chances that their small village will be overlooked, as it has been by governments of the past. It's not hard to identify with them. In a universe so vast, the small child in each of us might say, "How can I be found?" Even if there is someone or something that will come and collect me, how on earth—or maybe how in space—will they find me?

The sensation of being in space, of weightlessness, is sometimes reported to be one in which you feel that you're falling, which is the only natural way for humans to feel when there's no pull of gravity. And if there's no real up and no real down, that's not a bad description of what is actually happening.

It can get a bit scary. It seems to me that the only way out of the problem is simply this: to turn falling into leaping.

The existentialist theologian, Soren Kierkegaard, used to talk about something he called the "leap of faith". This was a leap that had to be made by everyone at some point in their spiritual lives. After you have read all the books, heard all the sermons and sung all the hymns, there remains this one solitary act. If you have been looking for the proof of God and Heaven, you have struck out. If you have asked the minister, the rabbi or the priest a hundred times for assurance, you have received nothing but opinion. At this point you have a few options. You could go on attending church or synagogue, trying to auto-hypnotise yourself into a sense of security. You could, as so many do, shrug and forget about the whole religion thing until forced to consider it in some future crisis. Or you could listen to Kierkegaard and take the leap of faith.

To take the leap of faith, it is first necessary to find the cliff edge. This isn't something you can do in your spare time. It involves a lot of thrashing about in the undergrowth of life, taking blind alleys and avoiding mirages in deserts. To reach the abyss takes a lot of living. It means being restless within your life, experiencing a feeling of incompleteness with the ordinary rewards of existence, a sense that there is something more than this. Often it will take the form of a life crisis—a bereavement, for example. The thing is, all roads lead to the edge, if you follow them long enough. There comes a time when it just isn't enough to have gilt-edged stocks and deluxe insurance policies.

The cliff edge may just pop up out of nowhere. It may be composed of the ordinary events of life. It may come at breakfast time, as in the case of W. H. Auden's poem where he says, "The crack in the teacup leads on to the land of the dead." It may come gradually, with ageing. It may come as a result of the innocent questions asked by our children. It may be ignored for a time, maybe a long time, but when it appears you realise it has never been far away.

Standing on the cliff means coming to the end of theory and speculation. However lucid your theories of life have been, however firm your grasp of biology and physics, you are faced with the unknown and unknowable. The abyss of uncertainty is there, an undeniable fact. Belief is not very helpful, because you have the uneasy feeling that belief was just a creation of the limited mind. What makes for pretty conversation in seminars isn't much use at the cliff edge. What you need is that most elusive thing of all: *faith*.

Faith isn't dependent upon theories and doctrine. That is just the wrapping we give it when we organise religions. Faith, we have good reason to believe, is a kind of perception, a sensing organ like your nose and ears. Where belief proposes, calculates and speculates, faith *perceives*. A good explanation of this is found in the Book of Hebrews. The writer, until the last century erroneously supposed to be Paul, says: "Faith is the substance of things hoped for, the evidence of things unseen." In other words, faith is not a concept but a perception. With it you have substance and evidence, not wishes and ideas.

Kierkegaard seems to be saying that faith comes only after a leap. You can't have it sitting on the firm ground; it is only available when you launch yourself into space. It isn't a weekend activity at all. There is a kind of lock on the door to faith that goes like this: you can't have it unless you take the risk that you'll find nothing at all. A lovely cosmic joke with an unknown punch line. It's only available when nothing else will do.

The Nigerian writer Ben Okri wrote a book a few years ago called "Astonishing the Gods". In one chapter he has a character stumbling onto the abyss, an uncrossable chasm. There is only one way across—an invisible bridge. This bridge is composed of mist, of light, of feelings. It can sometimes be glimpsed, but it seems too insubstantial to stand on. Yet, we are told, that is exactly what you must do. This is only possible when there is no other route to take. You have to be desperate to cross the abyss, which means you have to be well and truly fed up with all the diversions and detours of your personal history. You have to become exhausted with false trails and red herrings. The longing to cross over has to become very great, even greater than your fear. When you glimpse the bridge, you have the opportunity to cross. This might happen many times or only once.

Okri treats us to a vision of what happens to you if you don't cross the bridge, if you bottle out at the crucial moment. He says you will become half dead, half alive. What Okri is talking about is the soul; the errands of the spiritual path must be met and accomplished, or one has no life at all.

Okri and Kierkegaard both seem to be saying that it is somehow possible to *make* faith. You have to keep the bridge intact by walking on it. At each step it may seem too insubstantial to bear your weight. With each footstep it may be that your little scheming brain wants to say, "What?", and give up the whole thing. But each stride builds more bridge to step upon; it is the act of walking that creates the struts and girders out of mist.

This is more than challenging. This is the most crucial undertaking of all. We are being asked to take our small store of inspiration and trust and put everything on it. We are asked to do that if we are Christian, Jew, Pagan or nothing at all. We have to sift through the words of Jesus, Rumi and Marcus Aurelius and the observations from our own lives and cobble together a bridge-building kit. And we have to do it with no guarantees. None whatsoever, except for the inner whisper that grows louder as we get closer to the void. As the old circus expression goes, you are working without a net.

I believe that, as Hafiz said, "When the rider is ready, the horse appears." What we will need to cross the chasm is already there within us. It needs to become ready for use, and that is what the ups and downs of life are for. When we finally launch ourselves onto the bridge, we may find that it is not as insubstantial as we fear. The weakness, says Okri, is in us, not in the bridge. Our job is to overcome the fear by walking.

When you launch yourself into space, or try to tread on the surface of an invisible bridge, what you are really doing is calling the bluff of the vast and seemingly alien universe. You are calling time on all the ruses that keep you comfortable and—so it seems—spiritually empty.

What you find is not just rescue by some huge hand or a cunning engineering feat of beams and cables, but something infinitely more valuable. You are taking your place as a rightful inhabitant of creation, a child of God, if you like, and someone whose safety, whose belonging, has always been guaranteed. And in mid-air, you find that you are not falling at all, but soaring.

When life grows flat and empty, have a good look around. When the world betrays you, see if you can't spot a few beams and cables, made of air and feelings. When you despair, you may be only a heartbeat away from the bridge. And tell yourself, loud and clear, that it's time to move forward. That's the only game in town. That's why we're here, after all.

So, go ahead. Put one foot in front of the other. Stare down the big, bad universe and move onward, the way you were always meant to go.

WEEK EIGHT

Freedom is a Word I Rarely Use

In July (or perhaps Covid month four), my native country went through its annual eruption of fireworks, hot dogs and beer, to celebrate Independence Day. The parties went ahead as if there were no pandemic to worry about. Gun owners openly carried weapons as if they were demonstration placards. The rallying cry was the same: "Freedom!"

When I was a child, my father made a few half-hearted attempts to give me a lecture in history. I was told that all the wars we ever fought—even the one against the very country I'm standing in today—were done in the name of something called "freedom". I was never very clear about exactly what that meant, but I knew it was a good thing. I was also given the idea that we Americans had the world exclusive on it, had invented it, and were responsible for exporting it to all corners of the world. It was much later before I realised that the rebellious American colonists were talking about freedom from paying taxes, and not a lot more.

Since those days, I have come to understand a bit more of what it really means. It means I can stand up and say whatever I like, without fear of jack-booted secret police coming to arrest me. It means that, unlike in certain countries, I can fall in love with whomever I wish, and now I can even cement that love into a legal relationship. These things are all marvels, the luxury of a receding, benign period of history, things that we're so used to that we can hardly appreciate them.

But just at the moment, "freedom" has become the rallying cry for some darker forces. We have seen the re-emergence of a simplistic view of what freedom means, and the outlook is frightening. The present symbol of this is the face mask, which pseudo-patriots see as a violation of the absolute right to do as they wish. This insistence on the sacred rights of the individual equals a disrespect for community and simple fair play. So, it seems to me that it may be time to look closely at freedom and what it means, to untangle the Gordian knot that keeps humanity oppressing others, or worse, oppressing ourselves.

The word *freedom* has a few synonyms. *Liberty*, for example. My dictionary defines it this way: *the state of being free*, followed by this: *the power to do as one pleases*. The very words are thrilling, aren't they? This has got to be a goal worthy of struggle, hasn't it?

But there's something about it that bothers me. Maybe it's because it reminds me of the rhetoric I used as an adolescent, when I was straining against the boundaries of parental discipline. At that point in my life, I probably would have said that I wanted to do exactly as I pleased, that I wanted liberty from the shackles of oppression, shackles such as going to bed early on school nights and having to mow the lawn.

So, it seems to me that there is something adolescent—let us be kind and say "youthful"—about the notion of absolute freedom to do as we please. It is youthful in the sense that it seems to be arrested at the point of personal growth that makes an icon of things *individual*. This point of focus on things described as "I, me, my and mine" is perfectly natural and healthy—if a shade annoying—in teenagers; this is the time, after all, for separation from family and the formation of ego.

When it dominates in adult behaviour, it represents what M. Scott Peck called "the hole in the mind". This hole, the craving for absolute personal—or even absolute national—sovereignty, threatens human community, from the level of family all the way to international affairs. And because each of us is still on some level afflicted with adolescent desires, it is easy to manipulate people with statements like those made by a US president I can't bring myself to name from this pulpit.

A second synonym for freedom is *independence*. The dictionary yields some interesting definitions: *a state of… not (being) subject to control by others… not relying on something else… not looking to others for guidance in opinions or conduct…"* In absolute terms, what is being described is a state of being alone. This is the desert island fantasy—Robinson Crusoe writ large. In a state of absolute independence, you can do as you please, not rely on anyone else, take guidance and control from nobody. A libertarian, Boris Johnson dream. Problem is, it's a kind of devil's bargain; when you give up dependence, you might also give up friendship and mutual assistance. It gets lonesome being the only person in the world. Just think how glad old Robinson must have been to see Man Friday's footprints in the sand.

The first theological question asked in the Bible was "Am I my brother's keeper?" And, ever since, we have been looking for the balance between community and selfhood. It's been a long time since the American Revolution. But I can't help wondering how much longer it will be until—as an epidemiologist recently suggested—we celebrate something called "Interdependence Day".

I hope I'm not giving the impression that struggles for freedom are pointless or immature. There is tyranny and injustice. There are many people whose lives are blighted by dictatorship, poverty and debt. When these are present, there is no alternative to struggle. I spent a few years with some of these people in Africa and Latin America. The most poignant of which was the time I spent working with South African refugees.

My friend David Motshabe was a refugee from apartheid, caught in the net that tightened in South Africa after Steve Biko's death. I owe David a lot, because it was he who taught me how oppression works. He was a smiling figure, who always wore a spotless Panama hat, even—I am reliably told—in the bath. He had a soft, persuasive way of making a point, never raising his voice or using insult. He worked alongside me in a refugee centre, helping to make life bearable for a number of political victims. He used to steer me gently away from clichés about Third World politics, leading me toward a picture of global oppression, of which South Africa was just the most visible point. He believed that the liberation of South Africa would herald a shift in world consciousness.

I left Botswana, and David stayed behind. I had a term in the Dominican Republic, then in Kenya. We kept in touch occasionally—neither of us are great letter writers, and there was no email. I was surprised to hear from a mutual friend that David, his wife and new baby had been accepted in a resettlement programme in the United States. One summer I was working in a programme for Mexican migrant workers in eastern North Carolina, and I paid David a visit.

It was strange to sit with him in a red-brick, air-conditioned apartment near a motorway. He still had his hat. We drank iced tea and talked. I sensed that he had changed. He was working as a warehouseman, earning a low wage, but had access to welfare assistance. The level of luxury was higher than anything he had ever experienced before, and I naively assumed he would be glad. After a while he told me that life in America had taken the spirit out of him. He said that black people in North Carolina had achieved "freedom" at a level that South Africans couldn't have imagined in his lifetime, but that it wasn't good enough. He was suffering not only from subtle oppression, and the not so subtle oppression of racial politics in America, but from depression at the loss of a cherished myth—something that gave meaning to his life.

David's longed-for freedom, like the longing of the adolescent soul for total independence, doesn't really exist. Political solutions disappoint. Isolation palls. Could it be that this longing for liberty and independence is a masked desire of the soul for a different kind of freedom? Could it be that a refusal to need others is really a reflection of a thirst for a completeness that is unbearable in its absence? And could it be that the real obstacle to freedom, liberty, or independence is not only found in external oppressors, but in our own inner resistance?

Real freedom, suggest great spiritual teachers, lies not in overcoming one's external constraints, but in overcoming one's own illusions about oneself. Make no mistake: external oppression must be challenged. We are our brothers' keepers and our sisters' as well. But the front line is shifting location, moving inside. We have new battles to be fought against egotism, selfishness and childish fantasy—all in our own selves.

When the freedom train finally pulls out, I think that will be its new destination.

WEEK NINE

What We Do Not Know

Hey—I've got an original idea. Let's do something we don't do a lot of. Let's talk about God. Atheists, it's OK to cover your ears if you want.

One Thursday evening, I was talking to a man who came to see a film in our church. He expressed some curiosity about Unitarianism. I was explaining that, because we have no creedal statements, we have people with a wide variety of beliefs. Christians, yes, of the very liberal variety. Religious humanists, the odd Buddhist, a few Muslims, maybe even a Jedi knight or two.

"But I'm an atheist," the guy said, in that way I have heard so many times. Said as if it is still a radical position, and not the default setting of millions in the UK. It always makes me sigh. "You have everything but atheists," he went on. I had to gently correct him. I said, "Oh no. We have lots of atheists, and agnostics too, and sometimes everyone in the room is an atheist, at least for that day. Including me, the preacher."

Things have reached a point where the question, "Do you believe in God?" isn't really even asked any more. It's just assumed that no one does outside a small loony class and some diehard Anglicans, all over 80.

Why is that? Put simply, it's because the idea of God just isn't logical. You can't prove it. You can't build a giant Hadron Collider and capture a photo of a guy with a white beard. You can't even identify where He might live, even if He did exist. It's not logical, it's not scientific, so it's not true.

Now I think it's time for a disclaimer. Lately, with the rise of what is called the "alt-right", logic and reason have come under attack. Experts—or people who actually know things—are routinely dismissed. Not just by Bible Belt loonies, but by cabinet ministers and the president of the United States. A new entry in the OED a few years ago was "post truth".

So, am I doing the same thing, when I speak of a logic—and a reality—we can't yet see or understand? Well, no. I'm claiming the opposite. Where the "post-truth" crowd want you to believe something unreasonable—like global warming being a Chinese hoax, or vaccines being a plot by Satan—I'm asking us to do what Alfred North Whitehead called the greatest intellectual achievement of the 20th century: suspend judgement. Instead of filling our minds with absurdities, I'm asking us to keep them open, to watch for new truths as they emerge.

That's because it seems that there may be something we aren't able to see, but which has its own logic. Realising this, we have got two choices. One, dismiss what the voices of the sages have been telling us through the centuries, and cobble together some pale logic like,

"Well, that was then; we know a lot more these days." Or, two, let the riddle do its work on us. Let it be cause for second thoughts as we pass our days getting and spending, make us more ready to stop and watch the next time we pass somebody talking in what seems to be riddles.

Am I insisting that God does exist, despite logical evidence to the contrary? Well, no. Before I made any such assertion, I would have to ask you to define your terms. What do you mean when you say "God"? Are you speaking of the Old Man of the Sistine Chapel ceiling or some more mystical notion, having to do with spirit? Do you mean it like a metaphor, or as a statement of scientific fact?

No, that's not what I'm doing. What I am doing is introducing the notion that if there is one thing that can be demonstrated, over and over again, it is that we don't know what it is that we don't know. If we're unable to conceive of things like the parallel universes scientists keep turning up—I think there are currently four, by the way, or is it seven?—how would we recognise them when they bump into those of us still relying on textbook physics?

One way I like to think of it is to imagine a dog, a Labrador Retriever, say, looking at a poster on our church board. Next to her is a woman, her owner, also looking at the poster. The dog sees a green object made of metal and glass. And a white area covered in spots. Not very interesting, except perhaps as something to sniff for doggy messages. The woman is reading the words "Service at 11 a.m." Both are seeing, but the human, being of a different degree of awareness, is interpreting. If the retriever could think about it, she would think her owner was mad to be staring at the spots. Behaving illogically.

History has taught us that in each succeeding generation, things are brought into awareness that simply weren't there before. In recent times, outside of a few old Greeks, nobody much had ever heard of an atom, but within a blink in cosmic time, we were busily splitting them and creating a fearsome amount of energy, seemingly from nothing. Until they began to unravel the mystery of the human genome, nobody understood why someone could be the spitting image of their grandmother.

Maybe people like Jesus of Nazareth and the other great souls weren't being quite as illogical as they seemed. Maybe the illogic was ours. Being the equivalent of a Labrador Retriever, maybe we just didn't know what it was we were looking at.

I do understand how avowed atheists get to where they are. Despite some evidence to the contrary, I rely on logic myself. And when those apparently meaningless things we are all prey to surface from time to time, I can look up at the starry sky and see—not the home of God, but a vast, swirling, unfeeling cluster of gases and cold rocks. A cluster which doesn't care and isn't capable of caring about little me. In those times, the very idea of God seems like a cruelly debunked fairy tale.

But then something prompts me, and I think, "What do *you* know?" I hear voices from the past, saying, "Electricity is all smoke and mirrors." And "Man will never fly," and I tell myself: "What you don't know is far more thrilling and enormous than what you do. You may think of yourself as a fearless pioneer of the truth, but you really have more in common with the advocates of the flat earth theory. When you define the future in terms of the present, you always will get it wrong. You see, you don't know yet what it is you don't know."

Down there underneath the smarty-pants ideas I rely on, something prods me. Maybe it's the so-called "God gland" scientists have been looking for without success. Something wired into my nature that all the logic in the world can't quite make to shut up. I call it a hunch, like the hunch of detectives in novels. Or like so-called feminine intuition. Or like the faint hunch of scientists before they discover something that was there all along, but invisible to the unquestioning eye. You can call it faith, if you must. The author of the book of Hebrews, 1600 years ago, called it "The substance of things hoped for, the evidence of things unseen."

The next time someone asks me if there's a God, I won't get defensive. I won't waste time saying, "Well yes there is, but please don't confuse me with the fundamentalists, or the Pope." I'll say something like

LETTERS IN A BOTTLE

this: "I can't prove it, but I have reason to believe—good reason to believe—that someday I will know."

Someday we all will.

WEEK TEN

Breathe

Sometimes you hear some words that seem to make sense of the confusion with which we are surrounded. Those words are very humbling, to me as a person who uses words a lot, but also uplifting. So uplifting that I think they deserve repeating.

These words come from a TED talk given by Valarie Kaur, an American activist, lawyer and teacher who is a member of the Sikh faith. Her talk—available online—is called "Three Lessons of Revolutionary Love in a Time of Rage". The words that have most stayed with me are:

"What if this darkness isn't the darkness of the tomb, but the darkness of the womb?"

There is no one listening to me now who hasn't experienced darkness. Some of us listening now have experienced the kind Valarie Kaur was describing. I mean those of us who have had to flee our homes, who have felt the force of repression at first hand. But even for those of us who haven't suffered such experiences, there have been moments when we wondered whether it was possible to go on. Times of profound disappointment, times of illness and injury, times of loss.

That darkness that the speaker was referring to is the current mood in politics and society. It is in our streets. It seems to be everywhere. Something that all of us feel. As she says, it looks as if we have turned a corner and found ourselves in a crueller, more dangerous world. As W. B. Yeats said about his own time in "The Second Coming":

> *The blood-dimmed tide is loosed, and everywhere*
> *The ceremony of innocence is drowned;*
> *The best lack all conviction, while the worst*
> *Are full of passionate intensity.*

It's a time when there are plenty of candidates for blame. Public figures, important people in charge, billionaires, dirty cops, archaic laws; go ahead—you have your list and I have mine. We watch them as they say and do things we thought were no longer possible. We fantasise about action to bring them down. We feel contempt as well as fear. The only good thing about them is that we know who and where they are. Those people. The ones who are to blame. We have that much, at least, so we can wrap ourselves in virtue and wait for rescue. Never realising that the blood-dimmed tide doesn't just affect them. It has us in its grip, too. The darkness is shared, turning each of us in our own unique direction, farther from the light.

What Valarie Kaur said made me think again. What if it's not the bad people who are to blame, but the darkness itself? What if we were to realise that by locking horns with our perceived enemies we were only managing to strengthen the grip of that tide Yeats was talking about?

She makes that clear by pointing out that it's not just the tomb which is dark; the womb is sunless, too. The tomb, we think, is permanent; the womb is a stopover, a staging point for something brand new. Her prescription is one given to women in labour: "Breathe."

Anyone who has been following the news will recognise this word. It was the last one spoken by George Floyd as the life was squeezed from him by a policeman's knee on his neck. It is the most basic act of life itself. And if the darkness around us can be seen as the darkness of the womb, then the act of new birth depends upon the words of the midwife: *breathe*.

When she says "breathe", I take it to mean: slow down. Centre yourself in the reality of your own being. Detach from the impulses that want to turn you this way and that. It may be that, in the peace of this experience, perspective can return. From perspective, perhaps, understanding can develop.

Then she says "push". The next instruction of the midwife. I hear a call to positive action. That may take the form of marching in demonstrations or doing needed work with other victims of the darkness. It may mean writing letters to MPs or donating money. But I think, above all, it means the simplest, and yet the most difficult, response of all. I mean taking responsibility for the fate of the world, by challenging the darkness itself.

So how do we do this pushing she's talking about?

In recent times it *does* seem that things have turned uglier. It suggests that there is a kind of tide of goodwill that has surrounded us without our noticing it for most of our years on earth. Not that the harsh realities of the past were not painful and severe, but that there were certain elements—call them "core values" if you like—that went without analysis because they were always there.

My feeling is that there are things for which we have no name, perhaps things inscribed in our genes, that have kept an invisible medium of goodwill within reach. These are root ideas and feelings, so deep that they could hardly even be observed, that made up the field in which we humans have our being. Some things simply are not done. Some things are sacred. Some things will cause pain in the shrivelled conscience of a sociopath. These are the ideas that seem now to be at risk.

I believe that this tide that can sustain us or wash us away lives in the micro-world of everyday behaviour. That is solely and exclusively where it has its existence. No laws, government programmes, miracle insights can help this. Every one of us, in a very real sense, is responsible for the well-being of the world. If we can find a way to bless when everything screams at us to curse, we are moving partway into a new and less threatening world. If we can swallow our bile and frustration by acquitting an individual person of another race, an immigrant, a political opponent, a prostitute, from disdain for the whole of their class, we are indeed "pushing", bringing something new and possibly lasting to life.

Who is going to save the world? You are. You can go out from here onto the street, or get in your car and set out like old George Fox, the Quaker saint, "greeting that of God in everyone".

Your single candle can't light the whole room. But unless you light yours too, the darkness will remain. Those are the tricky mathematics of transformation. That's your mission, if you decide to accept it.

So breathe. Then push.

WEEK ELEVEN

Scaling the Wall

One day, I was in a taxi—where else?—and as usual, the driver asked me if I was Canadian. That's because British people seem to assume that if your accent isn't downright awful, you must be from a Commonwealth country. In reply, I confessed I was from the USA. He asked if I missed living there. I told him no.

"Why is that?" he asked, homing in on the subject. "Trump", I replied.

It was at that precise moment that I felt what I call "the Wall" drop between us. A few seconds before, we were two older men discussing harmless matters of accent and nationality. But after my comment, we were on opposing sides in a kind of mental war. As far as he was concerned, I had become one of "them", a climate-change believing, gay marriage supporting, remain-voting member of the "liberal elite". An enemy. And he had become a poorly educated, gullible dupe of populist propaganda, a turkey who would cheerfully vote for Christmas. An opponent. Maybe even an enemy.

He growled, "Why won't you people give him a chance?" He was talking about the president of the United States, a guy who talks about walls all the time. I heard: *you people*. 'You people' is an ugly substitute for some uglier names. *You lot* on the other side of this invisible Wall. The rest of the ride took place in stony silence.

I fear that the days of friendly disagreement are dead or dying. I worry that the reservoir of good will that made it possible has been swamped by a wave of suspicion and anger. It is possible to bump into the Wall almost anywhere these days.

I am no stranger to the Wall. I grew up in the American South. My family and friends were all racists. To be sure, they would have denied it. They were of the more genteel variety; the "N-word" was never uttered in our house. People like my family thought they were kind and liberal toward African Americans. The degree of sheer self-delusion in their attitude was exposed during the turmoil of the civil rights movement. I was on the other side from basically everyone I knew. That wasn't because I was born with some special moral genius. I had a series of lucky breaks and fruitful encounters that turned me into a liberal who marched in demonstrations.

The Wall descended on us. Any sort of meaningful conversation became difficult or impossible. I had become "one of them". It sucked all the love out of our house. It wasn't just politics. It was a matter of identity, of who we were. Descendants of slave owners, proud bearers of Southern culture, people of manners and—yes—breeding.

LETTERS IN A BOTTLE

Our house became a war zone without actual gunfire. My father assumed I had lost my mind and set up appointments with two different psychiatrists. But they soon revealed themselves as "one of them" too. They were Northerners, those intellectual phonies—Yankees. In the furious atmosphere of the Martin Luther King days, the Wall made it impossible to trust anyone with a certain accent. The shrinks said I wasn't crazy. I escaped to University, a liberal enclave in the Deep South, where my friends were all on the same side. My relationship with my family never improved, I'm sad to say, and the Wall still stands between those of us still living. So I do know about the Wall.

I felt the effect of the Wall when I worked with refugees in Botswana. I was working with Quakers, who used phrases like "reconciliation" and "peaceful resolution" in their brave, maybe Quixotic, efforts to end apartheid. In meetings with those on the opposite side of the Wall, I felt what might be sensed as a kind of force field surrounding them. There were subjects you could not mention. Interaction was cautious and lacked warmth. I was definitely "one of them" in that context, more so than my Quaker colleagues, with whom I occasionally quarrelled because they weren't radical enough.

What I know about the Wall is very much with me these days. Seeing it reappear is a source of pain for me. I left America during a time of conflict and division, and when I arrived in the UK, I felt relieved. For a while, I didn't sense the Wall here, even during events like the miners' strike and the Falklands War. But maybe I just wasn't paying attention. Now, in these particularly trying times, I do sense it, and it threatens to bring with it a mood of despair.

With the Wall, you make yourself safe among those who share your views. The enemy can't get in to spoil your day. But walls have two sides; you can't get out, either. Your apparent safety carries a price: you can become a prisoner behind your own Wall.

In times of conflict, such as we see before us now, the only real purpose must be not to win, but to bring a just peace, in which both sides can see the real goal, which is to make things better. It doesn't involve compromise with wrong-hearted points of view, but in introducing a new level of agreement that transcends selfish desires. It invokes the words of Abraham Lincoln: "The best way to get rid of an enemy is to make him your friend."

It is not easy. But what is, that has any real value? Besides, it is not a campaign that merely hopes for victory next November. It is more like a lifestyle, a dharma, if you prefer, a way of being that, for all that it may not result in the foreseeable future as world peace, is at least a step along the way. A tiny step, but a hugely important one.

When it comes to the Wall, which I fear we may all bump into in the days ahead, it means staying aware of the personhood of the opponent. It means instead of waging political warfare, an attempt to communicate on the personal level. Am I saying not to engage in action to change the world, through politics and rhetoric? No, of course I'm not; even if we don't want to go to the barricades, the barricades will find us. But unless we move toward what we conceive of as truth, justice and equality in a way which makes it sensible to ourselves and our opponents, we will only strengthen the Wall.

Being a blown-in-the-glass optimist, I saw in the early phases of the pandemic, and in its economic disaster tagging behind, a chance to reshuffle the deck. How much more so when the streets were filled with demonstrators for a rethink of policing, and more. I am still hopeful, but I have seen the Wall entering the picture once again. The real wall that has been erected around the White House, the barricades across city streets. And the metaphorical Wall as well. You know: real men don't wear masks. The right screams, "Get things back like they were!" The left says, "But things were screwed up before." Red states say don't worry about the virus; blue states worry too much. If anyone is right, I dread to think how we'll find out.

I think the best way forward is to refuse this game. Not to ignore it, because it gets played out everywhere. Just not to join it. If everyone is shouting "Which side are you on?", pay them no attention. It's all too easy to push your opponents into the status of enemy. When you see the enemy clearly in front of you, that's the time to watch your flanks. The errors of the opposition are lying in wait for even the most well-meaning of us.

The tired phrase goes, "We are all in this together." Often repeated by those whose desire is to restore our world to the unjust and unequal mess it has been in the past. But I would change the slogan a bit. I'd say, "None of us will get there until all of us get there."

I say it's worth the struggle. Don't you?

WEEK TWELVE

Coming Unstuck

We've all been stuck at home for a while now. Some with happier experiences than others. There have been increases in mental health issues and domestic violence. There has also been a surge in creativity, as people find new ways to communicate, work and maintain relationships. But everybody has shared one thing: we have all been stuck.

Here's a story about being stuck:

There was once a clever hunter who knew how to catch a racoon. It's a very simple thing: all you have to do is let the racoon catch himself. So, this is a story about a racoon who found himself in the strongest trap ever invented.

The hunter took a nice, juicy fish and put it in the hollow of a tree. A racoon came along and smelled the lovely aroma. Now a racoon is highly intelligent, but also very greedy. The opening to the hollow was just large enough for his hand. He reached inside and took hold of the fish, but when he tried to remove it, he found that the crack wasn't large enough to let his hand pass with the fish in it. He was stuck. He stood in front of the tree, unable to move.

A crow was watching all this from a branch. He fluttered down and said to the racoon, "I see that you are caught in the hunter's trap."

"Yes," said the racoon pitifully. "I cannot move, even though the hunter will soon come and catch me."

"It is the spirit of animals like us to be free," said the crow. "To run and fly unimpeded through the forest, to go where we will, like the wind."

"That is true," said the racoon. "I long for my freedom now that it has been denied me."

"Then why don't you release the fish and run away?" asked the crow. "There is so little time."

"Because it is also in my nature to love fish," said the racoon sadly. "My instinct will not allow me to let a plump, juicy fish get away. Try as I might, I cannot take my fingers off it."

The crow pondered for a moment, and then said, "The hunter will make your insides into a pie and your outsides into a hat. He will come along any minute now, and you'll wind up in the pot."

"What shall I do?" wailed the racoon.

"There is only one solution," said the crow, looking at the racoon's sharp teeth.

And that is why, in some parts of the world, they say so-and-so is as greedy as a three-legged racoon.

Everybody gets stuck sometimes, even without pandemics. We get stuck in situations that are as inescapable as the racoon's. You can hear people complaining that they are in a rut, or going nowhere. They will tell you about some of these: jobs that don't satisfy, relationships that trap, decisions that are put off until the opportunity slips away.

"Why don't you do this or that?" you might ask them. "Yes, but..." they will say. "Yes but" is like the jingle of the jailer's keys. There are always compelling reasons why someone cannot move forward. That's because they are doing it themselves, waking up at five in the morning, and like Hamlet, letting the tape of "to be or not to be" run endlessly around in their heads. The dialogue is between parts of themselves, each with its own imperatives and absolutes: security v freedom, love v comfort, struggle v rolling over and going back to sleep. The longing for material satisfaction vying in a self-defeating deadlock with the soul's need for fulfilment. And the trap is even cleverer than the hunter's because we carefully design it ourselves. The prisoner and the jailer are one and the same.

These traps we create are not just common. They are universal. Sometimes we are aware of them as problems, sometimes as blessings. But I believe that they are more than either. I believe that they are the very stuff of the soul's growth, the sirens and dragons and Cyclops caves of the pilgrim. They invite the divided parts of ourselves to merge toward integration. To find real awareness.

There are larger traps, ones that ensnare us all. Anyone who has been watching the events of the last few months in America will see evidence of that. We have been held in a socio-cultural trap of unfairness and inequality, best evidenced through the endurance of racism. When I say "we", I mean both sides of the issue—oppressor and oppressed. It is a trap that has stunted lives and arrested human progress. One of its important symbols—that of police brutality—has exploded into mass public awareness.

It may be that the months of inactivity and isolation have given us the chance to reflect, maybe to shuffle the deck of our ordinary lives. Being stuck has a positive face, because it can bring about transcendence. What else is a "stuck" place, a trap, than an invitation to change? Why else would we find ways to lose ourselves, if not to be found; to get stuck, if not to get free?

Here's another kind of trap, from a story curated by the Sufi, Idries Shah:

A certain locksmith fell out of favour with the king and was imprisoned in a cell. Because he was devout, he asked for and was given a prayer mat, woven by his family. Each day for twenty years he bowed in prayer five times a day, facing the holy city of Mecca.

One day the jailer found the cell door open and the locksmith escaped. Only later was it discovered that the blueprint of the lock on the cell door was woven into the pattern of the prayer mat.

There are 365 days in most years. Times twenty that's 7,300 days, plus a little for leap years, let's say. Five times on each one of those days makes a total of something like 37,000 times the locksmith bowed his head. Each time he placed his nose on the blueprint that would free him from imprisonment. That's a lot of praying, and a lot of scope for disappointment. When you're in a trap it's easy to get discouraged.

The patterns that confine us are not always visible. I heard one African American leader say during a television interview that "Most people who practise racism don't know they're doing it." Then, one day, you have a realisation. After 37,000 times of acting unconsciously, something seems to break through. What's happening now across the Atlantic is being called a "defining moment", an "inflection point". After 37,000 needless deaths and other crimes of unfairness, the death of a single man unravels the secret of the lock. The cell door is next, though we may struggle a while to find it. The stuckness of an entire generation promises a new way of life, and beckons us toward it. All of us.

If I had told you two months ago that being stuck in lockdown was a good thing, you wouldn't have been willing to accept it. If I had said that it would enable a different perspective on the larger trap that holds us all, even I wouldn't have believed it. That mass unemployment would enable millions of young people to head for the streets in mass protest. That the departure from the current order would reveal the inbuilt inequity of health care and income. That it would be possible to hear birdsong in the city and breathe unpolluted air. That the endless empty cant of politicians on both sides of the aisle would be showcased like the emperor's new clothes. If I had been wise enough to say any of these things, I would have been talking to myself, like a pavement madman.

One of the things I have most enjoyed as a minister is the discipline of talking to people with a wide range of beliefs. Those who believe in some sort of benign God and those who don't. Those who trust that the arc of history is bending toward justice, and those who only wish it were so. To both, I would now have to say that the visitation of these tragic times is carrying a secret treasure. We are in the midst of a profound sea change that is altering the terms of our reality, and freeing us—at least in part—from the stuckness in which we have been wallowing for a long time, maybe forever.

So, I'm looking forward to seeing what will emerge from this crisis, aren't you?

See you in the new normal.

WEEK THIRTEEN

Row, Row, Row Your Boat

Isn't it funny how we all know that little song? Everybody does. It appears in films and TV programmes such as Star Trek, in thrillers like Dirty Harry, and even in "Through the Looking Glass" by Lewis Carroll. Philosophers have used it as a departure point for enquiries into the nature of reality. It ends in the line "life is but a dream." You can bet your boots that it is being sung somewhere by children right now. But what on earth can it have to say to us grown-ups?

Because life isn't a dream. Or is it? That idea appears repeatedly in the spiritual literature of the East. In Hinduism, all these things we think of as real are considered to be the dance of Maya, or illusion. In Buddhism, all phenomena are caused by being stuck in an illusion, from which we have to free ourselves. If you were to ask an Australian Aborigine, he would tell you that we came out of—and go back into—a dream. The Dreamtime. Plato's whole philosophy depended upon the idea that what seems real is somehow lacking—like a dream.

But all the evidence of our eyes and ears tells us that this isn't a dream at all. If you drop something, it will fall to the ground, and it will do that every time, not like in a dream where sometimes it may not. Salt is always salty. Water is always wet. These are facts, hard, incontrovertible facts. Dream, schmeam.

But all that really means is that the elements of what we call reality are merely consistent. They always stay the same. Until recently, all aspects of our modern science were objective. Our need for scientific advancement had made us suspicious of subjective experiences; if you couldn't weigh it, measure it, describe it in detail in a PhD thesis, it didn't exist. End of argument.

It would have ended there if the idea of relativity hadn't popped into Einstein's brain. Once he started fiddling with things like the speed of light, we entered a new world of speculation. Things like if you leave Earth at the speed of light, travel around the universe and come back, you might arrive before you leave. Quantum physics took over: it's possible for a particle to be in two places at the same time. Yes, it is, even if no one understands why. All that consistency that we rely upon to prove to ourselves that reality is real gets lost. It occurred to us that reality isn't objective at all; it's subjective and infinitely variable.

When you look at a twinkle, twinkle, little star, you are quite right to wonder what you are. You're seeing the light from a star, light that left ten million years ago. You don't even know if the star still exists. Take a look at someone across the room from you. Do you see them right now? No—you see them as they were a tiny bit of time ago. The gap is infinitesimally small, but it's real. We don't even know what "now" is any more. Time loops and bends and curls, not just out there in the cosmos, but right here too.

It's hard to deny it: we live in a subjective world, not a fixed and unchanging one. You might even say that we live in a kind of a dream, in which everything is inside and nothing is "out there". Maybe that's what the ancient sages meant by our living in an illusion.

Sometimes, when I was a child, I had little moments, mostly while alone, in which things around me began to seem unreal. In those moments I seemed to be an observer who was somehow detached from my normal personality. The things that held reality in check—the familiar room, the sound of traffic, etc—were still there, but they seemed somehow to lose their power to anchor me. This was sometimes frightening, and the remedy was to rush to another room and talk with someone, engaging in some sort of normal activity. The sense of detachment would then fade. The observer me would hide under the fully engaged me, and I'd feel fine.

Now that would be good news, if all we had to do was just snooze through the dream, always heading downstream. It inspires me, because it speaks to me of a greater reality that we all inhabit, and that the pain and fear we must all go through may have a happy ending. But the little song we sang has got two parts. It also says we have to row, row, row our boats.

Have you ever done any rowing? A funny thing about it is that you don't get to face the direction you're travelling in. What you're doing is expending a lot of effort to move, and relying on fortune to send you in the right direction. I used to visit a spiritual retreat centre in South Carolina, where there is a large, beautiful lake and a rowboat for guests. I hopped into the boat one afternoon and decided I would row down to the centre library, where there is a place to tie the boat.

I hadn't done much rowing since I was a kid in summer camp. If I had ever known how to do it, I had forgotten what I knew. I rowed hard, until my hands were sore, and I couldn't help noticing that I wasn't making very much progress. What way I was making was all over the place, heading in one direction, turning to see where I was, and then compensating with the opposite oar. I did that until my hands were aching.

Not only that—I was embarrassed. People were watching from the shore, and I became convinced that they were laughing at me. I stopped in the middle of the lake and dipped my hands in the water. A few things began to come back to me. First, I was rowing too hard. My oars were slapping the water and being yanked out before giving me enough forward thrust. So I started doing what the song says, rowing *gently*, allowing the momentum to gather. My speed and my comfort picked up immediately.

Then I did something clever. At least I thought it was clever. I sighted from a clump of cattails to the place where I wanted to go by looking along an oar. Then I kept the clump over the same spot on the stern of the rowboat and rowed on what I would have to call faith, using—as it were—where I had already been to get to where I was going. It's always a good idea to let where you've been inform you of where you're going. Not only that; I started to enjoy it. I was almost disappointed when I felt the bow ease onto the bank, right in front of the library.

I haven't told this story in over forty years. I used to bore my friends with it, because I had a memorable experience out there on the lake. I realised then that rowing is about learning, more than about mere transport. So I think that is the inner purpose of the dream: using it to become wise. The real destination wasn't the library at all. It was the realisation that I had while doing it. That means the dream we inhabit is more than, as Ebenezer Scrooge tells Marley's ghost, "Just an undigested bit of pork." More than a pointless series of encounters and experiences. More than we dare to suspect.

Of course, all dreams come to an end, just as this one will. And the way dreams end is... what? Awakening.

I think this was best explained by Meher Baba, when asked what the purpose was of listening to the words of people who had managed to awaken from the dream. That's a definition of the great ones, the Sufi masters, what the Hindus refer to as *sadgurus*, the Buddhists as

Buddhas. That would mean Rama, Krishna, Zoroaster, Jesus and, yes, Mohammed.

Baba said to imagine that you are dreaming, and into your dream comes a figure who says, "Wake up—you're dreaming." Your reaction? "No, I'm not. This is real." And to prove it, you pinch yourself. But the figure, who seems oddly familiar to you though you can't remember having met, persists. You are dreaming. The only way you'll become aware of it is when you wake up, roll over and tell your bed mate or someone you see in the morning and say, "I had the strangest dream…"

So keep on rowing. Keep on until your wake-up call.

WEEK FOURTEEN

Spiral of Violence

One summer afternoon, while lockdown restrictions were temporarily eased, I ran up against an old problem. A problem which has bedevilled humanity from the days in caves to the chaotic time we inhabit now.

One glance at the headlines will demonstrate that we are living in a divided culture. Especially so in the US, where what is happening in politics has been described as a "cold civil war", but also right here, where the heating up of the Covid crisis has revealed some of the inequities we have thus far chosen to ignore. Poor people, especially minority populations, are getting poorer. They're getting sicker from the virus, too. And—it's obvious—they're getting angrier. This can be seen as something abstract, safely removed from our lives, or it can raise its head suddenly, as it did for me.

That afternoon, driving home, I turned right through a stream of traffic onto a shortcut. In the middle of the road were three teenage boys on bicycles, not moving. I had to step hard on my brakes. Two of them wheeled away with exaggerated ease, but one stayed in front of me, looking at me with what I can only call defiance. I waved my hand to indicate that he should move to the kerb, but he just kept a hard gaze on me. Cars were piling up behind me, and one of them honked his horn. I honked back, my blood pressure rising.

The kid turned his bike and drove directly at my front bumper, swerved at the last minute and, when he was beside my window, spat. The window was rolled up, luckily. He said a few choice things, and I did too. I swerved around him and went on, pulling in at the nearest safe stopping point to get calm. My legs were trembling a bit. I looked at the boy's saliva dripping down my window and wondered for a moment if I should call the police, or get out and walk over to the lad, grab him by the hoodie and give him a proper talking to.

But I didn't. It wasn't just the real possibility that he might pull a kitchen knife out of his pocket and stab me, though that did cross my mind. It was more a feeling that any reaction on my part would only make things worse. So, I sat for a moment and then drove on, aware that—like it or not—I was going to have to eat the feelings of outrage and fear that the boy had released into me.

I know that many people wouldn't have done exactly what I wound up doing. I know people who would have slammed on their brakes, jumped out of the car and confronted the boy. The image has a certain delicious lure to it: righteous anger at someone's wrongdoing. A sense of being entirely justified. Being able to say, "Go on, boy. Make my day."

But what would that have done? If the lad had been humiliated in front of his mates, you can bet that some other, perhaps even more violent act would have followed with yet another innocent stranger down the line. I would only have had the pleasure of telling everyone how I had achieved a small victory on Manor Road. My rush of blood would have brought with it a temporary feeling of triumphant virtue.

Two competing voices want my attention. One is that of a London cabbie, from whom I once got a tale of how "the coppers used to be able to bash hoodlum boys about the ear hole. We grew up knowing right from wrong." That voice, for all that it is crude and somewhat violent, is about enforcing a pattern of group morality that springs from the wisdom of the tribe. Bashing a kid about the ear hole is punitive. It relies upon an idea of society in which right and wrong are unchallenged and absolute. It hands back to the members of society the authority to judge and act. Simple and satisfying.

But the wisdom of the tribe is limited. It wants order and discipline, and scoffs at liberal arguments that would blame a poor background and abusive parenting for the kid's bad behaviour. It also would have—just a few years ago—insisted on jail terms for gay people caught having sex. It would have as its highest virtue a controlled world, where things that don't fit in are condemned and punished.

The other voice, perhaps surprisingly, comes from the New Testament. People like us don't pay all that much attention to Jesus and the Bible and all that. When we read that the young rabbi told people things like "turn the other cheek", we imagine that it was some sort of prescription for holiness. That if you did those apparently crazy things like giving your shirt away with your coat when someone asked for it, that you would somehow be earning brownie points with God, and that your payoff would come when you got to heaven. Those bits of advice, especially for those of us who don't believe in an attentive God, are so impractical that no one short of a saint could be expected to comply.

But what if Jesus wasn't talking about rewards in the sweet by and by? What if he was giving us clues about a very practical way of ending the vicious circle of violence, a method for making life better now, even in this pandemic-ridden world? I don't think the radical young rabbi has been given enough credit for his methodology.

The advice of the London cabbie—the ear hole basher—is to punish and control, and thereby to make things better. The advice of Jesus, you might say, is also to make things better. Not through discipline and punishment, but through stopping the wave of anger, recrimination and violence as it flows through us.

Some years ago, I was moved by the work of the Brazilian theologian and priest, Dom Helder Camara. He was part of the liberation theology movement of the 1970s and 80s. He wrote about something he called the "spiral of violence". In explaining why oppressed people rise up and attack their regimes, he pointed out that the rioting was actually not the first act of violence, but the second—that the violence had begun before the first stone was ever thrown. He was speaking of the violence that poverty and disempowerment wreak against poor people. America's recent experience of thousands of Black Lives Matter protesters in the streets is testimony to just this.

What I take from this is that violence is not a one-off act, limited to the moment, but part of a wave that travels through history and affects us all. The poison of the act the boy committed, and the poison of the anger and hatred that must afflict him every day, flowed from him into me. It has sat around for months in my head, fermenting, and now I'm sending it to you. You can help me now. Think about it. Did I do the right thing?

My own answer to that question is yes and no. Yes to the idea that I should simply accept the anger and pain of the moment, without acting in revenge dressed up as justified citizen outrage. I can afford it. It only hurts for a little while. That's not being Christ-like; that's being sensible. I might even get a sermon out of it, after all.

But also no—it wasn't quite the right thing to do. For the ripples of violence and anger to really stop flowing, there was something else I could have done.

My face must have borne the signs of the emotions I was feeling. I don't know what I said to him through the window. Something like "You can be arrested for that. It's assault." That not only had no effect on him; it might even have made him laugh. What I could have done was to respond in a way that would surprise him. I could have rolled down the window, spit or no spit, and spoken softly. Now I wish I had.

That's because I think it's not enough simply to let the event go unchallenged. I think the real value would come from what we might have to call a teaching function. By trying to show the boy that I had no feelings of anger toward him, I might have been able to drain a little of the swamp of pain where he no doubt lives.

Yes, of course you have to act differently if you come across a bully attacking someone else. And of course we can't go around being little pocket editions of Mahatma Gandhi all day long. But, having realised what ultimately has to be done, can't we remember the little cliché about a butterfly's wingbeat causing a hurricane in Europe, and just donate a little personal discomfort to the world? While we wonder what we can do to make things better, can't we at least try to say, "It stops here"?

WEEK FIFTEEN

Starfish Fools

I'm going to tell you an old story. It's not necessarily an ancient one, but just old because I know you've heard it before. Stories have a way of revealing meaning that expository prose can't, graphs can't, sermons can't. I'll explain what I mean by that in a moment, but for right now, let's just listen to the story.

An intellectual and a fool were walking in the same direction down a long beach. The intellectual noticed that every so often the fool would reach down and pick something up and throw it beyond the line of breakers. Curious, he approached the fool and asked him, "What are you doing?"

"I'm rescuing starfish," said the fool. "They get stuck on the beach and the sun dries them out and they die."

The intellectual laughed. "Tell me, how long is this beach, do you think?"

"I reckon it's about ten miles, more or less," said the fool. He picked up another starfish and threw it into the sea.

"And how often do you come on a starfish, on your walks?"

"Oh, lots of times. I guess there's one every ten feet or so."

"Let's say you're right. A mile is 5,280 feet long, so that's how many starfish?"

The fool smiled sheepishly and shook his head. "I never was any good at maths," he said.

"Well, I'll tell you. If you're accurate in your estimate, that means there are 528 starfish for every mile. If you multiply that by ten, the length of this beach, how many would that make?"

Once again the fool grinned and shook his head.

"Really!" said the intellectual. "You just add a nought on the end. That would mean there are over five thousand starfish on the beach every morning. How long does it take you to find and rescue each starfish?"

"Oh, I'd say about two minutes or so. I'm getting pretty fast at it."

"So, at two minutes each, times 5,000, do you know how long it would take to work this whole beach?"

"No," admitted the fool.

"Well, I'll tell you. It would take 10,000 minutes. That's 166 hours. How many hours are there in a day?" When he saw that the fool didn't know, he answered for him with impatience. "There are only 24."

"Well there's more in the summer time, I reckon," said the fool.

The intellectual sighed. "I'm trying to explain to you just how foolish your task is. You would need a team of ten men, working 16 hours a day. You couldn't possibly make a difference!"

The fool bent over, picked up a starfish, and hurled it into the sea. "Well, I don't know," he said. "But it made a big difference to that one."

We get that. We may not laugh every time we hear it, but we do intuit that there's a certain sense in which the fool isn't really a fool at all.

OK, maybe the intellectual went to the pub and told a few of his mates about the fool, and got a few laughs. Or maybe he said, "Oh, what the hell," and walked along with the fool for a while and threw a few starfish himself. Or maybe he did nothing at all and forgot the incident until the next time he found himself on a beach. But I like to think that the fool's answer lodged itself somewhere in the back of his mind.

In case you were wondering, I'm not up here today to discuss marine biology. The starfish story is dead on centre for a problem that has concerned me all my life. Here it is: how does the little action affect the big events of the world? How does what I do in private make any difference?

The slogan that sprang from sixties activism was "The personal is political." That conjures up an image for me of worthy people trekking to a recycling centre and putting bricks in their toilets to save water. It's not wrong, that phrase. But it doesn't get near enough to my core problem to make much difference.

That's not enough, is it? What is needed is change. Change in the structure that allows injustice. Change in the tired old slogans like "the deserving poor", "the workers and the shirkers", the "If you don't like it, go back home" responses of the winners and the would-be winners in the rigged game we're all stuck in.

So what do you do?

My advice is to become a prophet. Now, any first-year theological student can tell you that a prophet isn't someone who predicts the future. A prophet is someone who, as it were, predicts the present. That is, someone who is able to see clearly through the smokescreen of big words from politicians and who is not too groggy from distractions and pleasures to understand what is going on in the world around them.

One of the first prophets in the Old Testament was Amos, who denied being a prophet at all. He said he was a sheep-shearer and a pruner of sycamore trees. He lived a very long time ago—about 750 BCE. That was a time when Israel was flourishing, and the wealthy elite were getting richer and richer at the expense of the poor. They were extremely hard on immigrants, who were either kept as slaves or the equivalent. Amos was angered by the sheer scale of the injustice and spoke his mind. One of his great lines you may recognise. Speaking of the self-pride and over-the-top celebrations the rulers of Israel were fond of having, he said:

I hate, I despise your festivals,
and I take no delight in your solemn assemblies.
Even though you offer me your burnt-offerings and grain-
offerings,
I will not accept them;
and the offerings of well-being of your fatted animals
I will not look upon.

LETTERS IN A BOTTLE

> *Take away from me the noise of your songs;*
> *I will not listen to the melody of your harps.*
> *But let justice roll down like waters,*
> *and righteousness like an ever-flowing stream.*

Here's a modern version:

> *I can't stand your religious meetings.*
> *I'm fed up with your conferences and conventions.*
> *I want nothing to do with your religion projects,*
> *your pretentious slogans and goals.*
> *I'm sick of your fund-raising schemes,*
> *your public relations and image making.*
> *I've had all I can take of your noisy ego-music.*
> *When was the last time you sang to me?*
> *Do you know what I want?*
> *I want justice—oceans of it.*
> *I want fairness—rivers of it.*
> *That's what I want. That's all I want.*

Does that sound familiar? The wealth of the nations, little by little, winding up in the hands of a few? Immigrants disliked and ill-treated? Drivers pulled over and worse for the crime of being black? If it does, then you have a gift for prophecy yourself. Amos viewed himself as a free man, not as another chess piece in someone else's game. Whatever it was called, and however it was celebrated in officialese, truth is truth. Injustice is injustice.

Did Amos change the course of history? Nope. He got himself kicked out of Israel and wound up being murdered by a zealous priest. Not something I would recommend.

What I would recommend is carrying the truth around with you. Do you ever have those embarrassing moments in, say, a taxi, in which someone says something so racist and unfair that it shocks you? For years I just let things like that go by. I would think, "Well, I can't change his mind, so what's the point? Better to just get by." But I think I was wrong. The starfish fool in me is stirring. Now, at least, I say, "I'm sorry, but I don't agree with you."

You see, like the intellectual who met the fool on the beach, we're responsible to carry the load of seeing hopelessness and injustice and knowing it. Just like Amos, we have to refuse the comfort of being predictable and safe. When we see people getting killed in the street, we can't just shrug and leave it to our politicians. We have to, at least, let it change *us*.

Here's where we are right now. History moves in curious ways. Things stay the same, stay the same, stay the same for what seems like forever, and then comes what is called a tipping point. Maybe we're having one now in this pandemic. When that comes, everything does change. One more straw, and the poor old camel's back breaks. One more intellectual remembering the starfish fool, and the feasts and solemn celebrations Amos hated

LETTERS IN A BOTTLE

give way to something like justice, like an ever-flowing stream.

WEEK SIXTEEN

Finding Your Spring

There is a Sufi saying that goes like this: "If you want to know something about water, the last person to ask is a fish." I'm not kidding.

We residents of Europe think little about water, precisely because we are surrounded by it. From time to time there are drought warnings in Kent. Hosepipe bans are imposed, and the water companies make us feel guilty about washing our cars, while the companies themselves dribble away 40% of the supply with their leaky pipes. We take water so much for granted that it is difficult for most of us to realise that half the world worries about it all the time. I was once asked a poignant question by a teenager in parched Botswana: "Art, why does it always rain where the white people live?" I'm still trying to work that one out.

Most of the spiritual influences that have formed us have sprung from the desert places. They have made copious use of water and springs as spiritual metaphors. Moses struck the rock at Horah and brought forth a stream of living water in the desert; Jesus stood waist deep in the holy Jordan for his baptism; the Islamic conception of Heaven is—what else?—an oasis.

LETTERS IN A BOTTLE

Some years ago, after acquiring some land in the driest part of Spain, I went looking for a spring to supply my cabin with fresh water. There was another, older spring which, in the heat of summer, had slowed to a trickle and finally dried up. I suppose the metaphorical quality of this should have struck me then: springs do dry up.

Jacob Trapp, in his essay "Primitive Religion: Return to the Springs", speaks of finding fresh outpourings of water for the renewal of the spiritual life. This becomes necessary when—as happens from time to time—the truths of one generation become the absurdities of the next. When a vision is provided through the spiritual insight of a Jesus or a Buddha, the waters of that vision will be developed by devotees, made into ornate fountains, landscaped and elaborated until the freshness of the spring disappears and the water it produces is next to useless.

The wetness of the water remains: truth is—after all—truth, but in terms of their usefulness in quenching spiritual thirst, you might say that the springs run dry. This happens in real springs, and it does in metaphorical ones as well.

As I looked for a new spring for my land, I learned a few things about them. First, they appear in surprising ways. Because we cannot see beneath the soil to the deep structure of the earth below, we can only imagine what happens there. I have watched "water witches"—as diviners are often called—find water through the use of forked sticks and bent copper wire. The only difficulty is in knowing which diviner is reliable and which is not. Sometimes you can't spot a charlatan until you have dug a thirty metre well to no avail; the water witch will be in the next town by then, and you'll still have no water to drink. Some gurus, priests and prophets are like that, too.

As I looked for water, I found that there are clues given off by the earth for the truly observant. There was a patch near the path at the top of my land where a few strands of ivy grew, just a few feet from prickly pears and sisal plants. No water was reaching the surface, but the roots of the ivy—ingenious and tenacious—were finding it. I dug a bit and found mud. I dug a lot more, and hit dry patches. I decided I would have to change my plan. Finally, I began smashing bits of rock on the small shelf in front of me, and then suddenly water began to pour over my hands with the force of a bathroom tap. I can't tell you how I felt then, but it seemed to me like a miracle. In Spain, springs are called *nacimientos* or "births". It was just like that.

There are clues that life itself gives for the seeker of spiritual springs, and they are remarkably similar to finding water. The first is this: look in the damp and muddy places first. These are places within us that have about them a sense of emotional "dampness". They are sometimes the points of old wounds, old fears, old undigested experience. They are not clean and dry like so much of our lives. They might be places of embarrassment, of secrecy and denial. They might be the site of seemingly untenable desires or frightening images.

They are too muddy for walking in very often. And yet it is in these very places—the ignored and avoided regions of the self—where renewal often begins.

To get at the water of life, you have to dig, ruin your fingernails and sprain your back. It will fool you: there are a lot of false turnings and dead ends. A perfectly logical thing for the water to do is not what it seems to do. It will run around objects and hide itself with seemingly cruel caprice. You can find a trickle, and put your pickaxe into it only to find it has disappeared. You can start 12 inches above a small rivulet and dig all the way to Adelaide and the stream just won't be there. The water is where it is, and it has no interest in your inclinations or theories. With springs it is "take it or leave it".

Then, once you've found your spring, you have to find some way to use it. This can be tricky. You can do a lot with water, but you can't make it flow uphill. If you want to take it somewhere else, you've got to obey its instinct to flow downwards until it reaches the sea. I once tried to pipe some spring water to another small cabin a few hundred feet away. From where I stood I was sure the destination was downhill. I hooked up some garden hose and stretched it with great struggle through bramble bushes on a slope so steep that you literally couldn't stand on both feet at one time. When I got there, the water wouldn't flow. I rigged up a sighting mechanism with a spirit level and found that I had been trying—how like me!—to make water flow uphill.

We may have all sorts of complicated plans for the water that we find—actual and metaphorical. But I found by working with actual springs that the water has its own sense of purpose and that we are much better off adapting ourselves to it rather than trying to bend it to our will. Better to find a cool place in the rocks where you can dip your hand and drink when you need to than to exhaust yourself with pipes and pumps. Springs can be developed, water can be bottled, fountains can be built—but water, like the spirit, comes and goes in its own time and in its own way.

Maybe looking out at the damp landscape of England stretches this metaphor too far. But we are all pilgrims, really, sandal-slapping our way across a long stretch of desert, and we need a spring of cool water. Because the journey is long, we may be tempted to stay too long by an old fountain, even though its waters have long ago run out for us.

Visions come and go—they flow literally, as does the water. Because we are human, we may try to institutionalise—to trap—these visions, to make of them codes and rituals, and thereby rob them of their freshness. But the impertinent promptings of the spirit will send us on our way again, looking for and finding fresh sources of living water.

I hope that this place, even this online community, has become a place to dip your hand and drink when you are thirsty. For when this water is found we may discover how great our thirst has really been, and then we may drink deep for a long, long time. Even forever.

WEEK SEVENTEEN

Hunch Theology

Browsing through Facebook one day—in between having sublime and profound thoughts, of course—I saw a notification from a guy I used to know well. He is in his late thirties, a talented artist with a growing list of admirers. He has a lovely Spanish wife and is the father of two beautiful kids.

Here is what he said: *"What is the meaning of life? That's easy: nothing. There is no meaning to life. You are here because your mum and dad wanted children, or at least they wanted sex. There is no higher, deeper meaning to existence."* He went on to say that you should try to enjoy it, and if, possible, make it better for others.

I don't know why I found that shocking. A lot of my friends would self-identify as atheists, and I'd be lying if I didn't admit to having had atheistic thoughts myself over the years. I think it must have been the dismissive tone you so often hear with statements like that. Almost as if he means to say "Ha ha! Everything you might believe in is absurd and pointless."

We have good, loyal Unitarians in plenty who disbelieve in any sort of God, and their ideas are not only welcome, but often seductive. But I don't know any who are prepared to trash the idea of life having a meaning in any form. Even the hard-boiled genius Jean-Paul Sartre, father of modern existentialism, was able to cook up a concept of what he called "good faith" as a way of encountering the universe.

When you come out of a state of anxiety and confusion about the ultimate meaning of everything, it feels great. For the fundamentalist, it is the experience of being born again. They are enviable in one respect: everything they need is contained in one volume of two testaments. The Christian ones share this with the Muslims—everything you need to know is right there, chapter and verse. Never mind if the book was the result of political wrangling and infighting and has been edited to express the values of succeeding figures of power. You can overlook the bits where a presumably loving God suggests stoning gay people and exiling people who wear mixed fabrics. You can read it the way a child watches Dr Who—from behind the sofa. It is important to overlook inconsistencies, cruelties and nonsense, because what is at stake is that wonderful feeling of certainty, of knowing all there is to know about everything. Or at least knowing that everything can be known.

For the new atheist, things are similar. Each new quark and black hole discovered or indicated on a computer screen brings fresh proof of the accidental workings of the universe. Each trait newly attributed to genes brings a fresh dose of certainty, like a drip feed of painkillers. They are looking for a gland in the brain called the "God gland," which will explain away, once and for all, why the belief in a divine being is universal among human cultures. Down with God and all that; long live certainty.

In a following wind, you can forgive both of these positions. Uncertainty is uncomfortable. When certainty begins to slip away, we feel lost and desperate. That's why we cling so long to outmoded cultural norms, and why it is natural to resist change. That's one reason why the pandemic is so terrifying. If you have always been held fast by a culture, a network of family and society, and things happen which threaten to erode that security, you feel powerless and confused.

The forces let loose by the insights of physicists and mathematicians—let alone the new technology—have begun to erode the stable foundations of the world as we have always known it. There is a "paradigm shift" under way, and we are all a bit baffled. We can hardly hope to keep up with technology, and the days before Facebook have been lost. It is no wonder, then, that we will grab at any form of certainty when it comes along. In 1930s Germany, the Nazis offered a new myth and leader, but what they really offered was a route out of the confusion that followed defeat in WWI. Things are not so very different now, and it is already possible to imagine a new messiah or idea that would grip all but the wariest among us. During a pandemic, we are especially vulnerable.

Living without certainty is a hard path. The Unitarian slogan about "living in the questions" hardly scratches the surface. Forming a new theology, making a new formula to live by seems impossible in the stream of change we are all swimming in.

So how exactly do we live in uncertainty? If we are to avoid taking the first exit into a tightly fitting new strait jacket, how are we to manage it?

Here's what I would say to that most poignant of human questions. We can get by only through a single human trait. This trait is one we all share. The new-born infant cries at birth. You can see this—I do—as a prayer. Why would you cry if you didn't somehow sense there was someone there to hear you? What would be the purpose, even in the opinion of a committed Darwinist, of such a thing?

Of course, you might scoff at this. Say it is an alarm mechanism wired into us, a biological response to ensure care for a vulnerable creature. You can also say that a beautiful sunset is merely dust particles refracting sunlight. Or that a baby's smile when he first sees you is merely an evolutionary ploy to make himself too cute to leave on a hillside. You can say these things, but—go on, admit it—they don't feel right somehow. That points to the fine edge of our enduring mystery. And the only means we have to penetrate it is what I would call a hunch. A hunch which is the tip of a great iceberg of meaning shared, in its depths, by all of us.

I think we are all born sharing one thing. That thing is the capacity for trust. Trust that, whatever your degree of ignorance and helplessness, you are somehow held in a net of meaning that transcends theories and questions. It is a wired-in quality of us human beings. Justified or not, explained by some evolutionary cause or other, the question hangs there: why would we think that?

And yes, that leaves us where we started. Certainty simply isn't available right now, as we wend our ways through the twists and turns of life. But maybe we have a compensation. A deep-down sense that, whatever we discover—or do not—we are not lost. Call that faith if you wish. I call it a hunch.

My own hunch is reinforced by something quite simple. It was best expressed by the late Dr June Bell, a Unitarian from Edinburgh. At a conference one day, after some exhausting exercises in making and unmaking theology, she came up with this: "I'm from here," she said, "I'm at home. So I think everything must be all right."

WEEK EIGHTEEN

Do the Right Thing

Have you been following the US elections? I have, I confess. That's why my eyes are square, why I go around humming jingles from CNN adverts, and my best friends are starting to avoid me.

And each time some new perfidious act is revealed on the part of the "other side", I want to shout: "Why can't you lot just do the right thing?"

The problem is, ideas of what is right and what is wrong are as changeable as the fashions on the catwalks. What do you think your grandparents would say when asked if same-gender relationships should be honoured in law? Or that one's gender is a matter of choice? A new tide of relativity has washed over all our cherished values, leaving us feeling vulnerable in a time of upheaval that is so rapid that you need daily updates just to understand what you're seeing.

Sometimes, people in my kind of job encounter some tough calls on the right and wrong front. When I was minister at our church in Kensington, an elderly member of the congregation, who I'll call John, was slowly dying of congestive heart failure. He was in hospital, where his devoted wife, Mary, kept an eagle eye on him. They hadn't any children and had very few relatives, if any. I knew from past visits that they were—as they say—the whole world to each other.

At one point, John's heart stopped and he was, to all accounts, dead. They revived him with an electric shock and he went back to his side room after a day or so. Once, his wife left the room while I was visiting and he gestured that he wanted me to come near so that he could talk to me. He told me that he had felt odd since being revived, as if he were really dead, but being artificially kept from being aware of it. He asked me a penetrating question: "Art, do you think it would be letting Mary down if I refused resuscitation next time?"

I had just a few seconds to answer, because I knew Mary would soon be back. I thought about the devastation she would feel if he died, and I also felt the desperate weariness of the patient. One voice told me, "Life is precious and must be saved at all costs." Another whispered, "Mary has to accept what life has to bring." I heard Mary's footsteps in the corridor and I knew I wouldn't have another chance to speak to John by himself.

I gave him my answer. I won't tell you what I said. What would you say?

Was there a "right" answer? I felt a lot of things at that moment. I confess I was a little angry at John for asking me the question. I thought that nothing in my training had given me the sort of wisdom I would need for this situation. I confess I resented being someone who was thought to be a spiritual guide, because I certainly wasn't. And I felt something like fear, because I saw plainly that there is no rule book.

It would be nice to have a rule book. If the Bible hadn't revealed itself to be so flawed, we could treat it as the Muslims treat the Quran. As the indisputable and immutable word of God, Esquire, dictated by Him. But we Unitarians, and in fact most of the Christian world, can hardly think that anymore. It contradicts itself. It can be unbelievably harsh, so that I think that—if it were all true—I wouldn't want to live in that God's world anyway.

We hardly know what to teach children. If we teach values like fair play, absolute truthfulness, and modesty, we may be sending them out to play in traffic in a competitive, market-dominated world. If we teach values designed to help them get along with the society into which they were born, we may forfeit the emergence of the moral vision that has always characterised our heroes. By the same token, if we *show* them how we fudge our expenses statements or lie to annoying relatives, they may internalise this hypocrisy and have a loose grip on the truth. If we try to live in an artificially high-minded way, the strained nature of our lives may turn them in an opposite direction.

Society's view of morality and ethics usually underlines the desire for control. As Nietzsche sneered, "Morality is the rationalisation of self-interest." Those mores and folkways come into being to keep some sort of order in the dealings of people with one another. The so-called "Golden Rule"—doing unto others as you would have them do unto you—is pretty universal. Yes, a version of it does appear in the Bible, in Matthew, but it appears more often in most of the world's other religions, where it's been called the "ethic of reciprocity". But, like the law of karma, it seems a bit self-serving to me.

Enter the conscience. Like the soul, this little item in human beings is hard to find, and even harder to understand. Psychopaths, we are told, don't have one. Hitler didn't either, though he wept at the sight of flowers and little girls. George Washington had a huge one, because he couldn't tell a lie, or so the story goes where I grew up. We might imagine it as a kind of microchip set somewhere in the brain, a kind of default setting. But new generations of microchip come along every few days, making the old ones obsolete.

The whole landscape of morality and ethics, it seems, is a crowded jungle of ideas. You can't teach it, and you can't seem to catch it. It's not necessarily a part of your equipment when you come into the world, so you can't rely on some inbuilt valve or microchip. You can't memorise rules, because they are made to be broken, or at least reinterpreted in changing situations. So how do we learn how to treat each other?

If you look deeply into the world's religious writings and stories, you can find an answer peeping through. And it's simpler than we might imagine. Some things may need the treatment of philosophical high-flyers, but it's possible to look at human morality in another way. You may not be able to puzzle your way out of the moral maze; you may have to learn to trust your feelings. Morality contorts the mind but finds a safe harbour in the heart. So, I'll put it this way: doing good is not so much an idea as a state of being.

To see morality in this way, you have to turn to those whose paths led them to experience a very high degree of awareness, not just theorise about it. Of course, I'm talking about the mystics of all traditions, East and West: Hindu, Muslim, Christian, Jew, and nothing at all. With what must be considered a single voice, we are told that, as Meher Baba said, "You and I are not we but one." It is a simple but startling statement. The separateness that we feel is not what we truly are. In some way, we hear, all will be known as one being, who is most often called God. Here's how Julian of Norwich put it in the 15th century: "Our soul is oned to God, unchangeable goodness, and therefore between God and our soul there is neither wrath nor forgiveness, because there is *no between*." Between, according to the saint, implies that there are two distinct beings.

In virtually all religious traditions, you will find this idea expressed over and over again. When the threshold of the truth is reached, you find there not the ultimate other, but your own true self. This oneness is the reason, say the great ones, that love exists. Love is a kind of preview, or intuition, of the experience of oneness.

What this means is that morality is not a code, a rulebook, or a user's manual. It is a *sense*, like the other senses but one that can perceive facts that cannot otherwise be proven. When you are treating others with kindness, in some way you are treating yourself with kindness. And the feeling you get is like that when you are the recipient of kindness. When you are not cheating, stealing, killing others, it is because they are, in some dimly-perceived but no-less-actual sense, yourself. The words put in the mouth of Jesus, "Love your neighbours as you love yourself," could have easily been translated as "because he is yourself."

Meanwhile, we'll have to just muddle through, with no rule books, working it out slowly for ourselves. But that would be the whole point, wouldn't it?

WEEK NINETEEN

Paying Attention

Something very odd happened to me once.

I was at a campground at a US beach resort, having parked my camper van outside a launderette. I was using the telephone, because—believe it or not—mobiles hadn't yet been invented. I was standing at one of those semi-open phone boxes against the wall of the building, having a conversation with my wife. A woman in a yellow sports car wheeled into the parking space just across the sidewalk from where I was standing. Her brakes failed, and the car jumped the kerb and smashed the wooden wall where I was standing into splinters. Inside, washing machines were knocked over, and water jetted from broken pipes. The lower half of the wooden wall where the phones were was completely missing. The woman began screaming.

Without being at all aware of it, I must have seen the car approaching me out of the corner of my eye and hoisted my body upward using only my elbow on the shelf of the phone enclosure. I was wearing shorts, and my knees made a squeaking noise on the car bonnet as it passed. When it bounced backwards I resumed standing in the position I had been in. I remember saying to my wife that I would have to ring her back, as something odd had just happened. I looked around and people had come rushing from all over. They were helping the woman from her car, which had a totally destroyed front end.

I was completely calm. That is not at all like me, as I always run from the first sign of danger. I call it being sensible, but it has been called less pleasant things. The police arrived. Chaos reigned. People came over to me and asked if I was all right. I was fine; just a bit damp from the water that sprayed through the wall. I found another phone box and resumed my conversation, and as I was telling the story, I realised that I had had the narrowest of escapes. There is a parallel universe in which I have spent my life in a wheelchair, or died on the pavement at that campground. It took more than an hour for the shock to set in. I had to sit down for quite a while.

But before that, as I was walking back to my van, a man approached me. He looked at me as if I were the apparition of a saint. He had seen the whole thing, he said, and it was the most amazing spectacle of his life. He told me how I had just calmly bent my legs and allowed the car to pass under me, and how I hadn't even stopped the phone conversation. He wanted to know if I believed in God. I told him that I usually did, although I didn't know much about Him. I could see that he was dying to ask if I had an angel, but he couldn't get it out. I think I said something inane like, "It wasn't my time." He kept staring and shaking his head and finally just walked away.

I have never understood exactly what happened that day. What is odd about it is that I have rarely even thought about it. That's because, in the moment it happened, it all seemed normal and of no particular importance. I felt sorry for the woman, who was so upset that she went away in an ambulance. I have sometimes wondered if that man who questioned me had become a born-again Christian or something. And if what I told him was actually true: that it wasn't my time.

Now that's just an interesting story. At least I hope it is. It's anecdotal, so it doesn't necessarily mean anything. It's the kind of thing you can tell in the pub, maybe. But it really happened, and because it happened to me, I have some thoughts about it.

The science fiction writer Theodore Sturgeon wrote about something he called "synapse beta sub-sixteen". To explain it, he gave the example of someone walking down some dark basement stairs, and tripping over an empty bottle. Death or injury loomed, but, at the last second, the man reached up and hooked a finger over a coat hanger left dangling from a pipe. The synapse, according to Sturgeon, is the best hope for humanity: finding some way to survive when all seems lost.

I'm left with the idea that it is possible that we all really know more than we allow ourselves to be aware of. A scientist, feeling the need to explain away everything that doesn't conform to one theory or another, might say that the event was a combination of peripheral vision, adrenaline and, maybe, a false memory of what actually occurred. I won't say he's wrong, only that he's missing the point. However you crunch the details, the fact remains that something incredible—let's go ahead and call it *impossible*—not only happened, but happened in a way that made it seem perfectly normal.

What does interest me, however, is that there may be a good deal more awareness within and around us than we allow ourselves to acknowledge. And that that awareness may be the key to this great puzzle we're all locked in. I mean the one about God, the universe and all that.

I go on a lot about the folly of trying to understand those things. Have you noticed? After hundreds of trips up here to this witness box we call a pulpit, you must have heard it more times than you wanted to. I quote Meher Baba: "Asking to understand God is like asking to see with your ears." We haven't got the right equipment to deal with issues that big, so we settle for a few creeds and theological positions that are designed to shut up the questions that plague humanity. We're so worried that these positions don't hold water that we'll do almost anything to defend them: fight wars, burn people at the stake, fly aeroplanes into skyscrapers. In that way we're exactly like the scientists who, despite having a reputation for experiment and openness, are just as zealous about trying to make facts fit the pattern of whatever theory enchants them.

Through all of this, I think, we are determined to limit ourselves. It almost seems as if we are following a script and are reluctant to ad lib. The incident of my escape from the path of the yellow sports car cannot be all that unusual. I'm sure we can find tales of similar events right here in this room. There are perhaps daily clues that we are not as limited as we believe we are, but we seem determined to ignore them. There are many more things around than Horatio can explain away with his philosophy.

That's a little window, you see. A clue. To me it means that the limitations of our own minds, our adherence to the script, if you prefer, isn't quite the prison cell it may seem to be. Can you believe in God? Don't be silly; it doesn't fit the script. Can humans learn to live together in peace? That's ridiculous; ask Darwin. And all the while, things that we cannot credit, things for which we don't even have a name, are just a whisker away.

When things occur that don't fit our normal patterns of belief, we have two choices. We can discount them, chuck them in the bin where UFOs and ghosts have to live. Or we can acknowledge that we don't know everything yet—and just be peaceful about it. More than that, without sacrificing our reason or our reasonableness, we can open ourselves to see a bit more of this amazing thing we call life. We can expect to be saved from a yellow sports car—or not—and have peace with both. We can follow the lead of Walt Whitman, George Fox, William Blake, and even John Bunyan, all of whom wandered through a daily buffet of miracles.

Those lives give me comfort. They speak of a reality that we can't quite see yet, but the existence of which we so far have no good reason to doubt. It gives strength to my hunch that, despite appearances to the contrary, everything is in place. Nothing is broken or lost. Finding the truth, as mystics have long told us, is not about learning anything. It's about seeing what is lying unnoticed all around us. And even if you find yourself in exile from the part of you that is able to peer past the limits of the daily horizon, it has not disappeared. It has not become impossible.

It's just a matter of paying attention.

WEEK TWENTY

Smile, Stupid

A man walks into his local coffee shop on a wintry South London morning. The barista says, "Good morning," in a bright voice. The man replies, "What's good about it?"

Yes, the man was me. I had the grace to say, "Just kidding," afterwards, but I could see the look on the barista's face, still a bit pale. She's from Macedonia, not New York, and acerbic comments aren't her cup of tea. You'd be right if you thought that I hadn't exactly made her day. Even the larger than average tip couldn't restore something that I think may be beyond price.

I'm talking about cheerfulness. You know—that thing that makes the window cleaner whistle as he works. The quality that—if possessed—makes even unpleasant things seem better, like when the dentist's receptionist gives you a little smile, or that sheepish look of apology from a lorry driver who has blocked traffic on a busy road. Cheerfulness from strangers is priceless, literally. It's a gift. And, during a pandemic, it may be the difference between recovery and defeat.

Politicians sometimes talk about the "feel good factor" being an important element of poll predictions. They're talking about a mood that's shared by a lot of people. While theorists rant that it is policies that get someone elected, the reality is that mood is much more significant. It's sometimes referred to as the *zeitgeist*, the spirit of the times. When people feel good, they get more expansive and optimistic, and good things can follow from that. But when a mood is negative, as when a large daily newspaper such as the Daily Mail spouts out-and-out lies about immigration statistics, what results is fear; not expansiveness, but contraction.

A mood can travel as fast as a virus. A little prompting, and a mood cannot just result from a pandemic, but virtually create one. Many years ago, my ex-brother-in-law from California visited me when I was living in the Midlands. I remember something he said that shocked me. He said, "How can you stand living here?" When I asked what he meant, he said, "Everyone just looks so unhappy." Now, he was from California, a professor of psychology and a weekend surfer, so some of what he said can be taken with a cupful of salt. And it was during the early years of Thatcher's government, and the miners were striking and getting their heads bashed by mounted police. It wasn't the proudest moment for this country. But what he said still affected me. For days I went around looking at faces, and it seemed to me that he had a point. There was not a mood of bonhomie and cheer on the pavements of Birmingham, as he would claim existed on the sunny sidewalks of Berkeley, California.

We tend to underestimate the power of mood in what happens around us. We have a belief that we should be able to function without yielding to airy-fairy notions of an emotional reality. The whole idea of the stiff upper lip is about control of feelings, or at least concealment for a greater purpose. Legitimate fear gets confused with cowardice and mercy with sentimentality. The virtual byword of the he-man is expressed in these three words: cool, calm and collected. "Keep calm and carry on": what a wonderful slogan! I have it on a coffee cup. Perfect advice if you're invaded by Nazis, but a shade lacking for ordinary living.

People who understand the power of mood can change history, do change history. The quality known as charisma is just that—being able to create and even control the moods of others. That makes it potentially dangerous, but sometimes life-changing. Compare Mandela and Mussolini to see what I mean.

How does mood communicate itself? That's something you spend a lot of your early years learning. Facial expressions, tone of voice, body language—these are the markers of the state of mind. You know how babies will stare at you on a bus sometimes? If an older person did that, you'd probably flee or call the police, but you automatically accept their stare, because you know that what they're doing is reading your face, and learning the language of gesture and expression in the most intense school there is. If you smile at that baby, what happens? There it is coming back, as surely as if you were gazing into a mirror, and there is nothing on earth more captivating than seeing a baby smile back at you. It would be stupid to deny that the baby "caught" that smile from you.

Lots of research has been done into smiling. Despite the scientific bafflement, quite a lot is known. An intriguing remark by the Zen master Thich Nhat Hanh set me thinking about it. He said something like, "The smile is the result of your joy, but it can also be the cause of your joy." Meaning that our outward presentation to the world doesn't just reflect our inner state, but actually determines it.

This explains why what I did in the coffee shop with the Macedonian waitress was not good. For me to believe that my mood was my own business and no one else's was not just incorrect, it was naughty. That's not the way things work. If it takes some psychologists in labs to teach me that, so be it. But there are other ways to prove it.

In the early 1950s, the people around the spiritual master Meher Baba got a big shock. He announced that he was going to close the ashrams, schools and clinics that had grown up around him and his message, and that he and a few friends were going to hit the road. All the relative comfort that had evolved over years was to be scrapped. They were going to become a band of roving mendicants, living and sleeping rough, begging for food, wearing the kind of simple clothes that in India would mark them as people of low caste.

So they did. His followers' relationship to their teacher was to change as well. He was to be considered just an ordinary fellow, not any sort of exalted personality. For several years, they hitched and walked and rode fourth-class rail for hundreds of miles. One of them died. They received abuse, but also kindness. Here's what stands out for me. The one thing Meher Baba demanded of his friends was to remain cheerful.

Think about that. Life takes a huge dip. Things that were simple have become very hard. There is nothing before them but the next day of discomfort and insecurity. And what does their soul friend and teacher ask them to do? Be cheerful. So they did.

About that, Baba indicated that cheerfulness was not just a fleeting mood, but a stance to take for the whole of life. He said that cheerfulness was the greatest gift one could give to one's companions, and, as such, was in itself a spiritual path.

If you ask someone who is depressed to be cheerful, you run the risk of belittling what is a serious condition. It sounds inane, doesn't it, to say "cheer up" to someone who is suffering? It's the wrong way to go about it, anyway.

What's the right way? We all have, as they say, our bears to cross. There are times when it seems impossible to ignore the slings and arrows of outrageous fortune, and it is tempting to become as melancholy as Shakespeare's Dane. But maybe we intuit that our path is difficult for a reason, and that overcoming difficulties has more to do with how we view them than any magic remedy for solving them.

LESTER

The thing to do is to get right out of yourself. Find someone—on the street, in a bus queue, in church—and give them something. Give them something that you can wring from your own heart that will help them, and in the echo of that gift, heal yourself. Are you going to heal the world? Maybe. They say the beat of a butterfly's wings in Brazil can start a storm in Europe. So who knows?

Do something stupid this pandemic. Do it even if they lock us down again. I will if you will. Smile.

WEEK TWENTY-ONE

An Attitude of Gratitude

Did you have to say grace before dinner as a child? I don't mean at school or at church functions. I mean at the family table, at home, with the same people who, only a minute before, had been scolding you about something. Sometimes you would have to be the one who said grace. Maybe you said this one:

"God is great, God is good; now we thank him for our food."

That was the first table grace I learned as a child. Those few lines constituted the minimum you could get away with before lunging at the French fries to keep your greedy little sister from getting big ideas. The prayer could be said in one long expulsion of breath. It bore the same resemblance to the meal we were having as does tipping the head waiter in a restaurant: a bribe paid for value about to be received.

Sometimes, when we thought we could get away with it, we said other graces, like this: *"Good bread, good meat; good God, let's eat!"* But that's still miles more respectable than this one I first heard at summer camp: *"Rub a dub dub, thanks for the grub. Yeeeaaaay, God!"*

Did we think it was funny, making a little prayer like that? Because, if we thought about God at all, it must have been when we tried to bicycle atop a log over the creek, when the possibility of death made a rare, half-real appearance in our lives. Or when Granddad died in his sleep, we tried to imagine him being interviewed up yonder by a kindly but strict old man who knew precisely how many times you had prayed in your life, including *"Now I lay me down to sleep"* and table graces. God liked to be thanked and flattered and congratulated, just like Mr Simmons, the school principal, did at commencement days.

Were we grateful? Did we know we were lucky when we had extra gravy or pumpkin pie? And did we equate a continuing supply of good things with folding our hands? Probably not. Even the grown-ups' most usual prayer was not one of real thanksgiving at all, but said, *"Lord, make us truly thankful..."*, thereby indicating that we all really knew that gratitude was harder to come by than chocolate cake.

And yet, at this distance, the prayers seem to make more sense. It has to do with what gratitude really is, and how we humans experience it. It seems to me now that I had as a child the ability for a different kind of gratitude, one that sprang spontaneously from my enjoyment of life and was capable of giving pleasure to the most demanding God.

The word "gratitude" has a cousin: "gratification". This means "a state of satisfaction". It has to do with the real enjoyment of experience and the ability to feel that one's portion is enough.

Sometimes a little of that lost experience comes back to us in special moments. Something ordinary and unregarded slips through the screen of our psychic numbing and touches the simple heart of us, the place where the child still lives. It is like a light going on inside, and we have a sense of the magical quality of life that lives, as Manley Hopkins says, "deep down things".

The theologians of what is called "creation spirituality" have a special take on gratitude. It has to do with making life into a celebration of the portions handed out to each of us from birth. That means even those who are not quite so lucky, for whom disability or poverty has been what we would consider an invitation to resentment. Yes, it is possible to relish even one's misfortune, as Victor Frankl, founder of a branch of existential psychotherapy called "logotherapy", discovered while being an inmate in a Nazi concentration camp.

Now it's beginning to look as if we're headed for another lockdown. Not a concentration camp, but just uncomfortable enough for us to risk losing our bearings and letting resentment and self-pity have freer rein than usual. We already know that allowing bitterness to hold sway isn't a good idea. But where to find a source of gratification during a mass epidemic? The answer to that, it seems to me, especially during a pandemic, has to do with the cultivation of an attitude.

This attitude is about one very simple quality: trust. It speaks of an inner conviction that, despite everything, things are all right. Not that you won't get sick, or lose loved ones, or go broke—that's almost guaranteed to happen. And not that what is happening isn't just random circumstance, and—even less—the revenge of a spiteful God.

The voices from the great mystical traditions say that life is *about something*. That is to say, it is not something that just happens, then ends, without consequences. One way to put this is that life is a kind of school. It is an experience of learning, above all. Not like a conventional school, with its twin ogres of "pass" and "fail". No diplomas are handed out upon its completion, and no future high-earner positions are the prize. Instead, a kind of buffet table has been laid for every child as soon as it opens its eyes.

The circumstances of one's life may or may not be ordained by some real or imagined past. The circumstances of one's life—everyone's life, be they the Sultan of Brunei or Helen Keller—contain the possibility for growth and—yes—transcendence. Even in a concentration camp—so it seems—the possibility of enjoyment of experience and its companion, learning, exist.

You may reasonably ask, "But what or who is learning, since life ends in death and, perhaps, nothingness?" I would answer this way. If you were able to know, to take that dim organ we so proudly brandish at the universe as a magic weapon—the human brain—and fully know what this was all about, you would lose the plot. Literally, lose the plot. The intensity of life lived, not with certainty, but with trust, would be lost. It would be like spoiling the plot of a good novel. Like telling the hero when he is struggling against great odds that all he has to do is flip over to page 450 and find out what happens. The character with gratitude knows that he or she will arrive at page 450 by and by, but that page 150 has its own potential for the cultivation of the soul.

Yes, you correctly perceive that I believe that there is someone in all of us who is doing the learning and growing. You can refer to this as the soul if you like, or the "real self". I think of it as a form of myself that is always present but rarely noticed, just because I am too busy with the details of the plot. I don't think this version of myself began when my mother's waters broke, and I don't think it will end when they close my eyes.

And I believe that sometimes, just sometimes, this version of myself makes itself known. Maybe in a moment of insight gleaned from the sight of a mountain dawn. Maybe in a barely heard refrain of some wonderful music, or maybe in hearing the words of someone who is fully awake. It is not surprising that the most overwhelming emotion at that moment I can describe only as *gratitude*. But, knowing that I will have to spend most of my time here not being aware of this other self, I realise I must learn to cultivate the supporting attitude of trust. Trust that one day I will understand. As the line says, not through a glass darkly, but face to face.

It may be that gratitude is still hard to find, even on the good days. I think then we should try instead for gratification, for feeling that life and its small pleasures are bountiful and inexpensive. If I were God, I'd prefer that to a little congratulation before the mashed potatoes. Wouldn't you?

I have never liked being asked to give the table grace at a function. This happens a lot to ministers, and they sometimes privately grumble about it. The next time it happens, I think I might say something like this: "Dear God, if that is Your name, give me the ability to appreciate this table and the table of life spread before me. Let me not miss it by my littleness of heart, and let that be true for everybody."

WEEK TWENTY-TWO

2020 Vision

Are you sitting down? I hope so, because I'm going to reveal something shocking. When I was 12, I got "saved".

The occasion was an evening event at the local junior high school called "Sermons from Science". I went with my friend Mike Fields and his parents. The preacher showed film clips of marvellous things, like a mammoth frozen in the arctic ice with fresh, uneaten grass in his mouth, proving the existence of the Flood. Lots of other things that were supposed to be "scientific".

Suddenly a wave of happiness overcame me. I felt the presence of what I reckoned must be God in the auditorium, where the amplified music was rising to a crescendo. And when the preacher asked who among us had felt the presence of the Lord and wished to declare it, my hand shot up. The hands of Mr and Mrs Fields stayed in their laps, as did Mike's, who looked at me as if I had lost my mind. Perhaps I had.

Those of us who had joined the Crusade for Christ were led into a room where we were prayed over, embraced and registered. I was given some sort of book—it seemed like a very edited edition of the Bible—

a membership card, and a paper cup of squash with cookies. When I got back to the Fields' car, they had been waiting for an hour and a quarter. They were clearly not saved. It was a silent ride home, but I didn't mind. I was saved.

I stayed saved for about a week. My parents started getting mail reminding them that their son was a Crusader, and had agreed to support the mission. The book they had given me was not only boring, it seemed very un-Presbyterian to my mother. My father growled. By the end of the month I was back in the grip of Satan, but—I must say—feeling pretty well for it.

That was an important experience for me. In some ways, I suppose, it gives me the right to be critical of the hysteria-inducing religious bodies, but it also leaves me with a touch of sympathy. The idea of being saved, of having all those annoying doubts erased forever, being—however briefly—filled with certainty; that is not an inconsiderable thing to be shelved as mere lunacy.

My sympathy for those churches outweighs my disdain, because—if nothing else—they clearly show what the human condition is like on the inside. We're born with the inbuilt ability to foresee our own deaths. We have a large brain, which makes us able to wonder—which is thought to be a good thing—but never find conclusive answers, which is not much fun.

Some of us veer off into dogma of one kind or another and grumpily defend our opinions to the last minute. Others of us ease the pain of existence through obsessions and addictions, from harmless hobbies to full-blown substance abuse. Some of us are overtaken by despair, medicalise the condition and fall into a self-definition of being unwell. And some—a very few—knowing that the mind and heart of humanity is vast, get down to work.

But where to start?

It's frequently said that we live in and through stories. We have reason to believe that the story we have lived in for the past two thousand years or so is changing, but that's another sermon.

A few thousand years ago, the stories people lived in were different. At the time of Zoroaster, an epoch of much war and destruction, people saw God as having an enemy. This made sense, because who didn't? Their story was one about Ahura Mazda, the universal force of good, and Ahriman, the force of evil. The struggle between these two forces was reflected not just in the way people worshipped, but the way they lived. The lens of the day, the way the universal light was focussed, had shaped their story.

When the Buddha came along, Hinduism had already paved the way. The world was an illusion, a complicated dance performed by Maya. The illusion was very strong, and so the way forward was to transcend it altogether, not just progress toward perfection, as Rama had taught. The story of the early Buddhist was the escape from the wheel of births and deaths through a refusal to participate in the dance. The goal was Nirvana, a state of non-existence that represented total liberation.

The Rabbi Jesus appeared at a time when the Hebrew world had been rocked by the events of the Maccabean war against the Greeks, when thousands of their young men had been killed, apparently contrary to the guarantees of Jehovah. What is worse, they were a subject state of the Roman Empire, ruled over by a puppet king from, of all places, Samaria, the low-rent district of the Jewish world. Jesus extended the ideas of the sect known as Pharisees, which promised a world after this one. Heaven was still a new idea to Judaism. With his insistence on a loving father rather than a stern king for a God, the charismatic rabbi focussed the chaotic light of changing times into a new story, one which affects us still.

Each epoch has had its story and its lens with which to focus the light of reality, or God. Human beings demand lenses with which to make sense of the world, and they can be protective about them. Wars are still fought because two cultural lenses focus the light differently. You don't have to go farther than Northern Ireland to see that.

The thing is, lenses are only useful for a while. The light changes, the world turns, and you find yourself squinting through lenses that are worn out. In my case, my reading glasses are getting a little stronger every few years. I only know it when I get a headache in front of the computer and find that I'm really not seeing very well.

Religious lenses, the means by which you focus the light of God, are just the same. What made sense in a former generation just doesn't work a little later. The stories shift, through events like World War I and the publication of Einstein's theory of relativity. The lenses we inherit just don't do the job for us, and we get spiritual eyestrain or even go blind.

There have been times in my life when certain religious lenses seemed, for a season, to work. I'm old enough to have been brought up in a more or less intact Christian culture. That's why I got saved. I used to be able to wear the Christian lenses, perhaps not with perfect comfort, but without terrible headaches. Sometime in my adolescence, I don't know exactly when, I needed a change of prescription. Later on, in my twenties, psychedelic substances and Eastern mysticism became the means by which I focussed the light. Then things changed again. So I put away my Hermann Hesse and Alan Watts books and read E. F. Schumacher and Herbert Marcuse. My need for lenses changes all the time, as my vision does, even if the one light remains the same.

I believe that we have used up our inherited lenses. Trying to peer through our granddad's spectacles is inefficient and painful. How he focussed the light with them suited his time, not ours. We need new pairs of our own if we want to see clearly again.

And I don't suggest we need to go around switching lenses all the time. Put on a pair of Sufi ones today, Christian mystical ones tomorrow, and Buddhist ones next week, and you are engaging in mere syncretism, and it will just make you dizzy. What I think we need to do is grind our own—take the pain and fear of our life and use it as an abrasive to grind the glass, then take the joy and love that is also ours and use its softness to polish the lens clear. I'm told that if you rub two glass discs together, one will become convex and the other concave. Maybe that's about relationships. But I don't think we can become a spiritual Bausch and Lomb and pass out standard prescriptions. Even worse, we don't want to be in the business of marketing trendy sunglasses that make everything look rosy. I don't think we can mass produce any lens at all. What we can do is to help each other grind our own, until we are all able to see clearly.

The reason I think we can do that is that I think we are at the point of growing up spiritually. That's part of our new story. None of us expect to find quick solutions, really. We are here in the world to learn. Our restless questions lead us on to our own glimpses of the truth, which is more than many-faceted; it is infinitely varied without ceasing to be one. That's what we're really doing here, in case you wondered.

So grind on. Halleluiah! AMEN.

WEEK TWENTY-THREE

We Have Lived So Long without the Holy

I wish I could see you this morning. Not just because I miss all of you, but because I'd like to involve you in my thinking about something. There's something here that deserves our attention. It has a name, which I'll share with you later.

I started thinking about this when my friend Lol told me about a recent conversation he'd had. Last year, having received some generous bequests, we had this whole church redecorated. The painters were good at their jobs, which shows in here now. One of those men has been back recently, to deal with the ceiling collapse on the stairwell. He told Lol that, when they were working here in the sanctuary, they found themselves singing hymns.

Now, I don't know which hymns they were singing. Probably not our carefully edited versions of old favourites in the Unitarian hymn books. More likely, they were memories dredged up from childhood mornings in assembly or Sunday school. What interests me is that something about the energy of this place evoked what I imagine are long-abandoned religious feelings. If these men are anything like the 96% majority of unchurched

Britons, it would speak of some deeply rooted thoughts and emotions that hardly have a place in the world we're living in. And something about the vibes of this room prompted the recognition of the *holy*.

When thinking this through, I realised that we spend very little energy these days attending to that word— *holy*. It points to a mindset that we might fall prey to; in order to avoid merely superstitious beliefs, or, perhaps out of a desire to avoid the strait jacket of creedal worship, we have allowed ourselves to become numb to those things associated with holiness. The world outside is agnostic. Only about 4% of us keep scratching about in the disused mines of church and worship, looking for nuggets of truth overlooked by the majority.

And yet the decorators sang. Could it be that there is a residual nesting place for things spiritual in all of us?

One of my favourite poems goes directly to heart of this. Philip Larkin worked as a librarian, but was a poet by vocation. He called himself an agnostic, but his public image was that of a fairly hard-bitten atheist. He worked hard at it. He kept an expensive Bible permanently opened on a desktop lectern, and read through the whole thing. He once declared, "How can anyone believe that utter nonsense?" (He actually used a different word, but I'll spare your tender ears).

He wrote his poem "Church Going" in 1954, when the decline in church attendance was in full stride. The institution that had been at the centre of rural English life had already fallen on bad times. There were empty churches, not yet turned into trendy wine bars, in every part of the country. Places you might expect Larkin to avoid.

But he wrote:

> *Yet stop I did: in fact I often do,*
> *And always end much at a loss like this,*
> *Wondering what to look for; wondering, too,*
> *When churches fall completely out of use*
> *What we shall turn them into, if we shall keep*
> *A few cathedrals chronically on show,*
> *Their parchment, plate, and pyx in locked cases,*
> *And let the rest rent-free to rain and sheep.*

When I read the poem, I go briefly to a time in my childhood. One day, early for choir practice, I found myself alone in the huge sanctuary of my parents' Presbyterian church. I had to get to the back stairs that led to the choir dressing rooms in the basement, and to do that, I had to walk past the big brass cross on the carved wood altar beneath the extravagant stained glass windows that rose to the ceiling arches. It was totally quiet; I could hear my trainers rustling on the carpet. I felt something unfamiliar: a combination of wonder and—yes—fear. Later, I discovered that those two words define a third one: *awe*.

As I passed the altar, a sentence popped into my head. I mouthed it silently as I passed: "God lives here." In that moment, it seemed to be true. True in a way that trumped other things I thought I knew, and yet totally unbelievable. My childish mind was overwhelmed, and within ten minutes, I was being lectured by the choirmaster for singing late. The hymn was "Holy, Holy, Holy".

What that tells me now is that there is a corner of our heads in which the concept of the holy is alive and well. Because it doesn't tally with all the secular information we have gorged on, it lives like a creature in hibernation. Only sometimes, when the conditions are exactly right, does it assert itself.

Philip Larkin lived and died an agnostic. I have always been grateful to him—one of my favourite poets—for not taking the hard line of atheism. Being an agnostic, someone who acknowledges that he doesn't, cannot, know the truth about God, The Universe and all that, he felt impelled to stop in that particular church. And just for a moment to feel things to which he was not accustomed. He writes:

A serious house on serious earth it is,
In whose blent air all our compulsions meet,
Are recognised, and robed as destinies.
And that much never can be obsolete,
Since someone will forever be surprising
A hunger in himself to be more serious,
And gravitating with it to this ground,
Which, he once heard, was proper to grow wise in,

LETTERS IN A BOTTLE

If only that so many dead lie round.

A church where I ministered some years ago was designed as a multi-purpose space, with an eye to renting it out as a money-making activity. In fact, the first time I ever visited it, I was attending an event that had nothing to do with Unitarianism. It is a lovely, large space, and plenty of deeply spiritual moments have occurred there. I liked it when I was resident minister, and I still have a fondness for it. But it never evoked in me the feelings that made the housepainters sing.

It is true—and doubly proven during this lockdown—that a church is not its buildings, but its people. But, as I discovered later on various journeys to India, the devotion shown by generations of pilgrims enhances the atmosphere of holy sites. It seems to soak into the very walls. That is why I'm glad that we rarely rent out the premises these days. When I was finally able to come back into the church after two months' absence, I felt it at once. The years of seekers seeking, doubters safely doubting, people singing songs of praise beautifully or off-key. I felt—let me just go ahead and declare it—the presence, however dim and remote, of the holy.

I believe that we can live without many things. Without romantic love, without financial security, even without family, though that is more difficult. But I have come to believe that touching that seat of the holy buried within us is essential. Essential in its original meaning: *of the essence.*

It makes me believe that a necessary part of being human is finding that element within us, an element that can drive us to our knees. Maybe it's a cathedral. Maybe a country walk. Maybe even the statue of Sir Alex Ferguson outside Old Trafford football ground.

Whatever it is for you, I hope you bring it along next time you're allowed to come into this place. We'll all be waiting.

WEEK TWENTY-FOUR

Frequently Asked Questions

Does anyone in this liberal place recognise this book? You might recognise it as the thing Donald Trump held up at that Washington church after clearing away protesters with tear gas. The Bible. I had to study this scrambled collection of truths, lies and political polemics for two years when I was in ministry training, only to find that it was hardly used in the churches where I preached.

So, it's tempting to dismiss the Bible as merely a collection of outdated myths. But some of it has a surprising ability to do what any good work of philosophy relies upon. It poses questions.

In Genesis, third chapter, Adam and Eve have been enjoying the Garden of Eden—and maybe enjoying it too much. One afternoon, after it had cooled down, God takes a stroll in the garden. He finds them hiding in the shrubbery, wearing fig leaves, and asks why. They explained that they were ashamed because they were naked. So God—stormy Old Testament version—says, "Who told you that you were naked?"

The jig was up, and the whole sad tale about eating the fruit of the Tree of the Knowledge of Good and Evil, along with the cunning serpent who caused the problem, came tumbling out. What followed was punishment—banishment from the happy life inside to a hard world outside. Gone was the fruit falling from trees and a life lived in happy innocence. Adam had to work for a living by the sweat of his brow, and Eve would have to experience the pain of childbirth. There was another outcome to the sentence, too: it gave reason for the historical church to blame women for just about everything.

They call that "the Fall". But maybe it wasn't all bad, after all. The Eden myth talks about a time when humans stopped being unconscious animals and became beings who were aware of themselves—self-conscious. They were able for the first time to conceive of death. They were self-aware, just as we are.

I always think of the irony contained in the use of this story by creationists to dispute evolution. It is in fact a story *about* evolution, the evolution of consciousness, a journey of human beings away from their roots in what is called the "lower orders" of life. As in physical evolution, the change was not just inevitable; it was a victory.

Or was it? Being conscious carries its problems, as we all know. The ability to anticipate the future brings with it not just the ability to plan and do things. It also brings fear with it. It brings the night demons at five o'clock in the morning. Being self-aware is the root of all human anxiety. The question: "Who told you you were naked?" was the gift and the burden of humanity. The gift of reaching understanding, not just perceiving. The burden of knowing you will die.

The second big question appears in the next chapter. Adam's sons, Cain and Abel, are out working. In a fit of jealousy, Cain kills Abel. This is no idle reference; Cain was a herdsman and Abel a farmer. The dispute over land use was alive and well at the time when the Bible was written. I have seen this enmity myself in northern Kenya. We see it in Western movies, too—the cattlemen versus the homesteaders. But God wants to know where Abel is, so he questions Cain. His laconic reply has been the springboard for an awful lot of theological reflection ever since. He says, "Am I my brother's keeper?" Another way of saying that is the question: "Do I have a moral responsibility for other people?"

The former Unitarian minister at Cambridge, Frank Walker, once wrote an article for the Journal, "Faith and Freedom", that has stayed with me. In it, he asks us to imagine walking along a road and hearing a baby crying. Looking in a ditch, we see a tiny infant, wrapped in a dirty blanket, lying on its back. So, I ask you: what would you do?

Right—not much confusion there; we would pick up the baby and take it to some agency that could help. At worst, we might be forced to take it home. But Walker points out that such natural-seeming behaviour only began about the time of Jesus. Not belabouring the connection, he just points out that rescuing the infant is a modern idea. A Greek citizen of those days, in the same circumstance, would look at the child and think that, sad though it is, the baby was probably left there by some grieving mother who could not take care of it. Knowing that, she simply left the child to the hands of whatever god she believed in. So, the ancient Greek would walk on by.

So, here's a non-Biblical question for us: what do we do when we see the suffering of Syrian and Yemeni children on our TV screens? I say this to point out that the ancient Greek in us is not yet dead.

One explanation for this, I suppose, is that curious phrase: "compassion fatigue." Compassion fatigue is probably inevitable. At first, events and images shock you, stun you, make you sick. Then, because we are nothing if not survivors, the images lose their potency. The same thing happens in real life situations. I have talked to people who were in wars who say the same thing. What horrifies you at first sight becomes familiar, then commonplace. If it weren't so, we wouldn't be able to cope. It probably has to do with a release of endorphins, or some other hormones they'll discover next week.

And, since we can't go through life unable to cope, something gradually changes in us. We get tougher, more able to withstand terror. We begin a long process of what James Hillman calls "psychic numbing". We wind bandages around our tender psyches to muffle the ups and downs. As we get older, we begin to say things like "I don't care." Even though this is frequently just an exercise in bravado, it is also true. We care less, feel less. If we are lucky that's how we navigate that minefield known as adolescence. That's why the sweet-natured child of yesterday can become the indifferent teenager of today. The innocent child can become a school bully. The abused child begins abusing others. The most normal kid can become capable of shocking cruelty.

Alongside this numbing process we are growing our identities as members of society. We become socialised into groups and families. We internalise the logic and ethics of the social unit. We know right from wrong, if only because we have memorised it by rote. We know what brings censure and what brings praise. We believe in decent, humane values, fair play and even the Golden Rule. The horrible pictures of gassed children in Syria merely spoil our dinners a bit.

But do we *care*? Do we really, really care if someone we don't know gets Covid-19? Do we care when a seven-month-old baby in a country we have never visited dies of simple diarrhoea? When time runs out for some damaged soul in a Texas death row cell? And if we don't, why not? What's the matter with us?

The verb "to care" is defined like this: *To feel trouble or anxiety... to feel interest or concern.* The key word in this is repeated: "to feel". That's where care leaves behind rule following. It starts where behaviour ends, because it's not about what you do; it's about what you feel. And feeling is what we set out to get rid of when we started winding our souls in protective bandages, when not feeling pain or grief or fear seemed like a good idea at the time. What may have been necessary for survival turns out to be a loss of that most human trait of all—feeling.

Our defences are our greatest burdens. Whatever techniques we evolve to keep ourselves from pain wind up creating more of it, but we can't feel it because we're numb. Somewhere our souls might be screaming, but we don't hear them because we're deaf, too. And we can't see what's in front of our eyes because we filter everything through the cracks in our fingers, the way kids look at horror movies.

That's why the second big question has hung around for all those centuries, surviving dogma and redaction, and still sticking out of the folds of history like a wounded limb. It follows out of the first, because it implies that our burden and gift of awareness leads to the question, "Am I my brother's keeper?" Responsible for the baby in the ditch? For you?

Cain asked that question with a shrug. But isn't it a bit too late for shrugging? If we're going to survive, don't we need to answer?

WEEK TWENTY-FIVE

Remembering the Future

Remembrance Sunday, November 2020

There is something about November. I'm not sure what it is, exactly, but its effect is unmistakable. It could be the sense of the final drawing in of the year, the last shreds of kindly warmth stripped from the days, the ruthless time change bringing dark down on us like a soul curfew.

November also seems to be the season of sorrow, following on the heels of the celebration of ripeness that is October. The bells tolling out the mournful tones that announce the annual revisiting of the horrors of war are also markers of the passage of time slipping through the fingers of the world.

I had nearly forgotten about Remembrance Sunday, I confess. The pandemic has so scrambled time and the ordinary routines of church life that it might have slipped by unnoticed if I hadn't seen the poppy pins on the TV presenters' lapels. Then my thoughts turned slightly from my focus on lockdown.

This year portends an even more bitter taste of morbidity. The pandemic has stubbornly displaced the normal elements of our lives, and has left an unexpected shadow over everything. Lockdown is back with a vengeance. The pale faces of political leaders wear expressions you might expect if we were in an actual war.

In normal times, thousands of old men and women would be gathered a few miles from here, remembering times past, times that have flowed away so gradually that they are almost unnoticed. But each year there is a pause, a collective hush, and we feel the weight of memory—even if we did not live through the commemorated events themselves. Remembrance Sunday is a time machine as resolute as Christmas, but with a different feel. This day, at least in part, is about early, possibly senseless death.

Poets such as Rupert Brooke and Stephen Spender bring back to us each year why we subject ourselves to such an orgy of grief. The shock of the war in Europe was such that it is asking a lot of any society to brace themselves and move on. The whole thing hangs upon a promise we made (you know the one): "At the going down of the sun, and in the morning, we will remember them."

Keeping that promise is costly. Not in terms of expenses from the Exchequer, but in the currency of human life—in the way we feel about ourselves. The memory of the youthful dead haunts but, it seems, does not really inform us. Are we stuck? Have we cast in amber a moment of our history that bids large to define us?

And how is it that we have apparently forgotten the flu epidemic that followed on the heels of the Great War, leaving behind even more early deaths than all the battles of the conflict itself? There are no rows of graves with identical markers to commemorate what happened in the thousands of ICU wards, and is happening again.

That question has led me to believe that we need a shift in perspective. That instead of being riveted to the past we need to learn to remember the future.

If this sounds like merely playing with words it is because as a society we tend to forget the prophetic statement made by George Santayana: "Those who do not understand their history are condemned to repeat it." That's a paraphrase, but it's near enough.

On almost any news programme these days, you can find those dreadful images of wounded children, of hospitals and schools blown apart, of families made to scratch in the rubble for enough to eat. Recently, I was watching a television interview with a Syrian boy of maybe ten, disabled by war wounds that had only recently healed. He was a cute kid: smart, articulate and attractive. He spoke enough English to make the interview interesting.

I tried to imagine him as an adult, and then saw others in the frame of the shot. Young jihadis. Young men bent by fealty to unrealistic slogans and—above all—twisted in anger and hatred for the distant perpetrators of their victimhood: Russian, Kurd, Syrian nationalist, Al-Qaeda, ISIS and American.

LESTER

The impulse was to save the boy, heal his lesions and fractures, rebuild his school. But what was being asked for, in the higher councils and in the devastated streets, were tools of war. A new rain of death on the Enemy, whoever he might be. As the child said, "We will kill them all, inshallah." That is, if God wills it, we will pour tragedy on their side as they have poured it on ours.

Just for a moment, I caught a glimpse of the Enemy. It seemed to be a little parcel of hatred, kid-sized. We were tucking it into his arms as we once gave him his lunch. So that when the hour rolls round, he has his small necessities: vengeance, anger, hatred.

Now you can see something of that same hatred in places where adherence to ideology or cult leaders has divided the world. It is no less striking, and, we fear, no less dangerous. It is the poisonous offering of the pandemic that has magnified what was a problem into a crisis.

Our services and our cultural memories today are full of the images of lost youth. Our fitful declaration is to remember, to never forget. And while we are remembering these poor lost children, our parents and grandparents whom we never knew, we are preparing a new crop of glorious victims, "martyrs", as they are called. That is the highest calling and ambition for so many: not to prevent the new appearance of the glorious dead, but to become them.

It would be so easy to become cynical, if we had not already seen faint glimmers of hope in recent history. For the first time, nations actually discuss what is and is not allowed. Despite the fact that this is honoured more in the breach than the observance, it is just possible to see a tiny advance in awareness. Maybe we're on the right track; a long one, but, like the arc of justice, bending in the direction of peace.

These words contain the single most important question we can ask ourselves. They ask, "Are we improving?"

That's why I suggest that we stop remembering only the past, so full of hard lessons, but also of victorious jubilation. Is it possible to remember a future that hasn't happened yet? It was that which flashed before my eyes while I watched the news programme.

Maybe we'd have to create a new colour for the poppy. A rainbow one? We would certainly have to find new ways to occupy ourselves on days like this. Public improvements, maybe? Parties?

But what we'd seriously have to do is a kind of alchemy. We'd have to learn to turn the heartache of the past into helpful and life-sustaining activities. Most of all, that alchemy would have to happen in ourselves, by looking at the world as something that can be newly organised, newly imagined, newly created.

At this century's remove, we have a chance to see, open-eyed, what we must learn from history. See clearly, or—as George Santayana said—be condemned to repeat it. We are older now, and hopefully bigger, and the demand of our past is clear.

So let us remember them rightly. All those who fell in the great reaper of war: the aunt who died in a cattle car or a camp, the father who died before we left our mother's womb, the marine private surprised by a sniper four days after the surrender, the accidental casualties of friendly fire, the brave soldiers and the secret cowards, the innocents of Coventry and Dresden, the builders of the bridge on the Kwai River, the maimed of Hiroshima. The innocents bombed in their sleep in Palestine and Yemen, the victims of the suicide bomb in the crowded market, the many, many millions now in flight from their homes.

Let us remember the front-line workers, no less heroic than the men who streamed out of the trenches into machine gun fire. Let us remember, in the words of Joe Biden, those who face empty chairs at the kitchen table.

Let us remember them, and in so doing mark this time as a threshold and as a source of revival. This is no dusty history lesson, but a vital lens by which to view our lives. It is there before us to use, to make changes that will increase our claim to being human.

And so, yes, let us honour the promise we made. Let us remember well. Let us remember the future, our future. Then let us change in the ways we know we must.

THANKS

No book, even a slim volume like this, is the work of a single person. So:

Thanks to Steven Appleby, for his advice and the cover design. To Phil Appleby, for helping my words make sense. To Steve Dick, who produced the filming sessions from which these pieces were taken. To Lol Benbow, stalwart and indispensable assistant in the production. To Gill Stone and Will Higgins, whose music lifted the occasions. And to my patient congregation, who have listened while I learned for the past 14 years.

ABOUT THE AUTHOR

Art Lester grew up reluctantly in the American South. After working for several years in Africa and Latin America at village level development, he returned to the UK, where he trained as a Unitarian minister. For the past thirty years, he has served congregations in England, Ireland and France. He is the author of seven books, including the award-winning *Seeing with Your Ears*.

In Memoriam:
Reverend Stephen Wilkins Dick

Printed in Great Britain
by Amazon